Sunday School Specials 2

by Lois Ke[ffer]

Grou[p]

Loveland, C[o]

Dedication

To our folks,
who have held the hope
and lit the path.

Sunday School Specials 2

Copyright © 1994 Lois Keffer

Credits

Edited by Candace McMahan
Designed by Dori Walker
Cover designed by Liz Howe
Illustrations by Randy Kady, Jan Knudson, and Jeff Carnehl

Unless otherwise noted, Scriptures quoted are from The Youth Bible, New Century Version, copyright © 1991 by Word Publishing, Dallas, Texas 75039. Used by permission.

Library of Congress Cataloging-in-Publication Data
(Revised for volume 2)

Keffer, Lois.
        Sunday school specials.

        1. Christian education—Textbooks for children.
2. Bible—Study and teaching. 3. Christian education of
children. I. Title.
BV15561.K38 1992   268'.432   91-36923
ISBN 1-55945-082-7 (v. 1)
ISBN 1-55945-177-7 (v. 2)

11 10 9 8 7 6 5 4 3   03 02 01 00 99 98 97 96

Printed in the United States of America.

Contents

THE LESSONS

Introduction

Wow! Yea, God!

Those are the most appropriate words I can think of to express my gratitude for the response to *Sunday School Specials*. Letters and calls have come from Kenya, from American Indian reservations in Canada, and from all across our country telling how kids and adults have enjoyed using the lessons in *Sunday School Specials* to learn about how God wants them to live.

So here's *Sunday School Specials 2,* with all my best wishes and prayers for lots of great learning ahead!

Once upon a time there was a Christian education director who dreaded summer vacation. It's not that she objected to fun in the sun and that sort of thing—the problem was that when vacation arrived, Sunday school became exceedingly unpredictable. One week there would be eight kids in a class, and the next week there would be two. The following week somebody would bring 10 cousins, and kids would be hanging off the rafters. And, of course, the 10-cousin Sunday would be the day all the other teachers were out of town. What to do?

One day a very bright person in the congregation said, "Let's put all the kids together and do some kind of creative Bible lesson with the whole group." And then a series of wonderful things began to happen. Kids began to look forward to Sunday school because they knew it wouldn't be the same old out-of-the-book stuff. Little kids liked getting lots of attention from big kids. And big kids liked helping out and being looked up to.

The teachers really got into it, too. Everyone signed up to teach one or two Sundays. The rest of the summer they could join an adult class or take some much needed R & R.

In fact, the concept of combined classes went over so well that the adults got a little jealous. So she set up a couple of intergenerational lessons each summer and let them join in.

"Why save these combined classes for summer?" the teachers asked. Why indeed? So she began using combined classes whenever holidays, absences, or in-between Sundays presented a strategic dilemma.

The joyful, memorable learning experiences in those combined classes gave birth to *Sunday School Specials*—and now to *Sunday School Specials 2.* In this new book you'll find a whole quarter's worth of creative, combined-class Bible lessons you can use in the summer or any time at all! Each lesson contains an opening game or activity that grabs kids' attention and gets them tuned into the theme; an interactive Bible story; a life application activity and a reproducible handout that help kids apply what the Bible says to their own lives; and a challenging, meaningful closing.

This book includes a section on celebrating special times. These five lessons cover

Thanksgiving, Christmas, New Year's, Valentine's Day, and Easter—but you can go right ahead and use them now. Everyone loves Christmas in July, and giving thanks is certainly appropriate any time of year! The lesson on new beginnings can apply to a new calendar, a new school year, or a new summer together. And any time is the right time to celebrate new life in Christ.

Within each lesson we'll let you know what to expect from kids of different ages and give you tips on how to get kids working together. Group's hands-on, active-learning techniques make it easy for you to capture and keep kids' interest. And you can be sure that the Bible lessons they learn will stick with them for a long time. The "Time Stuffer" section shows you how to keep kids productively occupied before and after class and during their free moments. And you'll find special tips for gearing each Bible lesson to meet the needs of your particular group.

You have in your hand a wonderful tool that can help you solve your Sunday dilemmas. So go ahead and try something new. We want to help you make your Sunday school special!

Lois Keffer

Active Learning in Combined Classes

Research shows that people remember most of what they do but only a small percentage of what they hear. Which means that kids don't do their best learning sitting around a table talking! They need to be involved in lively activities that help bring home the truth of the lesson.

Active learning involves teaching through experiences. Students do things that help them understand important principles, messages, and ideas. Active learning is a discovery process that helps students internalize the truth as it unfolds. Kids don't sit and listen as a teacher tells them what to think and believe—they find out for themselves.

Each active learning experience is followed by questions that encourage kids to share their feelings about what just happened. Further discussion questions help kids interpret their feelings and decide how this truth affects their lives. The final part of each lesson challenges kids to decide what they'll do with what they've learned—how they'll apply it to their lives during the coming week.

How do kids feel about active learning? They love it! Sunday school becomes exciting, slightly unpredictable, and more relevant and life-changing than ever before. So put the table aside, gather your props, and prepare for some unique and memorable learning experiences!

Active learning works beautifully in combined classes. When the group is playing a game or acting out a Bible story, kids of all ages can participate on an equal level. You don't need to worry about reading levels and writing skills. Everyone gets a chance to make important contributions to class activities and discussions.

These simple classroom tips will help you get your combined class off to a smooth start.

● When kids form groups, aim for an equal balance of older and younger kids in each group. Encourage the older kids to act as coaches to help younger students get in the swing of each activity.

● In "pair-share," each student works together with a partner. When it's time to report to the whole group, each person tells his or her partner's response. This simple technique teaches kids to listen and to cooperate with each other.

● If an activity calls for reading or writing, pair young nonreaders with older kids who can lend their skills. Older kids enjoy the esteem-boost that comes with acting as a mentor, and younger kids appreciate getting special attention and broadening their skills.

● Don't worry about discussions going "over the heads" of younger students. They'll be stimulated by what they hear the older kids saying. You may be surprised to find some of the most insightful discussion coming literally "out of the mouths of babes"!

● Make it a point to give everyone a chance to shine—not just the academically and athletically gifted students. Affirm kids for their cooperative attitudes when you see them working well together and encouraging one another.

How to Get Started With *Sunday School Specials 2*

Lesson Choice

The lessons in *Sunday School Specials 2* are grouped in three units, but each lesson is designed to stand on its own. You're not locked into doing the lessons in any particular order. Choose the topics that best suit the needs of your class.

Several of the lessons contain suggestions for using an intergenerational approach—inviting parents and other adults in the congregation to join the class. You may want to schedule these lessons for special Sundays in your church calendar.

Teaching Staff

When you combine Sunday school classes, teachers get a break! Teachers who would normally be teaching in your 4- to 12-year-old age group may want to take turns. Or, ask teachers to sign up for the Sundays they'll be available to teach.

Preparation

Each week you'll need to gather the easy-to-find props in the "You'll Need" section and photocopy the reproducible handout. Add to that a careful read of the lesson and Scripture passages, and you're ready to go!

Time Stuffers

What do you do when kids arrive 15 minutes early? when one group finishes before others do? when there's extra time after class is over? Get kids involved in a Time Stuffer!

Each Time Stuffer needs just one preparation—then it's ready to use all through the summer or whenever you're teaching these lessons. Choose the Time Stuffer that best appeals to the interests of your group or set up all three!

Care Cards

You'll need envelopes, masking tape or tacks, markers, and note paper.

Have students each write their name on an envelope with the flap open and facing toward them. Tape or tack the envelopes to a wall of the classroom. Place markers and note paper nearby. In their free time, encourage students to write or draw positive notes to other kids and tuck the notes in the appropriate envelopes. Be sure to make an envelope for yourself, too. You'll enjoy getting fan mail as well as writing encouraging notes to your students.

Group's Discover-It Bible Map™ Hunt

You'll need *Group's Discover-It Bible Map™*, markers, and 3×5 cards.

Post the map on a classroom wall. On separate 3×5 cards, write challenging things for kids to find on the map. For example, you might write, "What was the name of the mountain where Noah's ark came to rest?" or "How many camels can you find?"

When kids have a few minutes to fill, they can wander over to the map, take on a fun and interesting challenge, and learn more about the Bible!

Vacation Board

You'll need a cork board, picture postcards, pushpins, and palm trees cut from construction paper.

Mount the cork board at a height that's easily accessible to your youngest class members. Decorate it with construction paper palm trees and a few scenic postcards.

Encourage kids to bring in postcards, brochures, photographs, or drawings of places they have visited. Kids will have fun sharing their experiences and finding out about what their classmates have been doing.

Learning to Know God

God in First Place

LESSON AIM

To help kids understand that ★ God deserves first place in our lives.

OBJECTIVES

Kids will
- examine how they set priorities,
- learn why a rich young man chose not to follow Jesus,
- identify interests that may compete for first place in their lives, and
- make a commitment to put God first.

YOU'LL NEED

- ❏ five plates of treats
- ❏ five paper grocery bags
- ❏ a "treasure box"
- ❏ slips of paper
- ❏ a pencil
- ❏ Bibles
- ❏ photocopies of the "God Is First" handout (p. 17)
- ❏ scissors
- ❏ crayons or markers
- ❏ tape

BIBLE BASIS

Mark 10:17-27

Many of Jesus' teachings challenge our minds and our sense of fairness as we attempt to understand them. The story of the rich young man is certainly one of those.

A sincere, respected young man comes to Jesus full of admiration and enthusiasm. He addresses Jesus as "good teacher," then goes straight to the heart of the matter: "What must I do to have life forever?"

Good start! Jesus' response is almost a retort: "Why do you call me good? Only God is good." Jesus isn't going to make this easy. Perhaps Jesus is warning the young man that flattery and emotion won't get what he's after. Jesus proceeds to name five of the commandments—those that deal with people-to-people relationships. You can almost see the light in the young man's eyes as he says, "I have obeyed all these things since I was a boy." Then Jesus lovingly issues the challenge: "Sell everything you have, and give the money to the poor. Then come and follow me."

The young man responds with stunned silence. Then he turns and sadly walks away, unable to part with his wealth and put God first in his life.

Matthew 6:33

Jesus challenges his followers to want God's will more than anything. Those who succeed in putting God first can trust God to take care of all the other things that so easily command their energy and attention.

Putting God first is a choice. It's never easy, but it's always the right choice—and the benefits are eternal.

UNDERSTANDING YOUR KIDS

Many things compete for first place in the lives of your kids. And those things may not be all bad! Older kids may be concerned about having top grades, being the best in sports or music, and identifying with the "in" group at school.

Younger kids may still be in the "me first" stage—what they want at the moment is most important; all other considerations are secondary.

Kids of all ages may be consumed with the desire to accumulate the most awesome collection of whatever toys or gizmos are the latest, greatest things to have.

Our challenge as Christian teachers is to show kids that God and God alone is worthy of our first loyalty. Good grades, medals, championships, and possessions may bring pleasure for a time. But in the eternal perspective, those things may become dangerous roadblocks preventing us from giving our very best to God.

This lesson will help kids evaluate their priorities and understand that ★ God deserves first place in our lives.

The Lesson

What's First?

Before anyone arrives, set out five plates of special things such as quarters, strawberries, chocolate kisses, gummy worms, and sticks of gum. Cover the plates with heavy paper grocery bags and don't let anyone peek! Plan to have at least two treats for each person in the class.

As kids arrive, tell them they'll get to choose from the items on the plates, but they'll have to wait their turn. Line kids up from the youngest to the oldest. When everyone is in line, remove the bags and let everyone see what's on the plates.

Say to the first child in line: **Go the table and take one thing. Then go to the back of the line.**

Explain that kids can choose one thing from the table each time they come to the front of the line. Encourage children to go ahead and eat their treat if they've chosen something edible. Keep going until everyone has chosen two treats.

Then gather kids in a circle and ask:

● **How did you decide what to take first?** (I took what I like best; I took a quarter because I can buy something with it later; I took gummy worms because they're gross.)

● **Was it easy or hard to decide what to take? Explain.** (It was easy because I really love strawberries; it was hard because I like everything.)

● **Would you agree that all these treats are good things? Then why are there still things left on some of the plates?** (Because you said we could only take two things; because the things that are all gone were better than the things that are left.)

Say: **Sometimes it's hard to decide between what's good and what's best. Even though most of you like all the things I put up here, you had only two choices, so you had to decide what to take first, what to take second, and what not to get at all. In real life we have to make choices about what comes first, too. Today we're going to learn that ★ God deserves first place in our lives.**

A Rich Young Man (Mark 10:17-27)

Say: **Our Bible story today is about a young man who was rich. Let's explore what it would be like to be rich.**

Bring out your "treasure box"—it can be a jewelry box, a decorated tin cannister, or a wooden box of any kind. Choose an older child who's a quick writer to be your scribe. Give your scribe a pencil and several slips of paper. Choose a younger child to hold the treasure box and put the slips of paper in it.

Say: **Let's name all the things we can think of that a rich person today would have. Our scribe will write down everything we say, then we'll put those things in our treasure box.**

Children may name things such as millions of dollars, a big house, lots of cars, a swimming pool, and designer clothes. When children have contributed several ideas, pick up the treasure box and hug it. Ask:

● **How would you feel if you had all these things?** (Great; happy.)

● **What would you do if someone told you to give all these things away?** (I'd laugh; I'd say no; I'd ask why.)

Say: **Let's see what happened to the rich young man in today's story.**

Choose two good readers, one to read the words of the rich young man, and one to read the words of Jesus. Open your Bible to Mark 10:17 and have your readers do the same. Explain that you'll take the role of the narrator. Be prepared to cue your readers with a nod of your head when it's time for them to read their parts.

Begin the reading. Stop the person who's reading the words of Jesus in the middle of verse 19, after "You know the commands." Ask the class:

● **How many of the Ten Commandments can you name?** Although Jesus does not list all Ten Commandments in this passage, it will be a good review for your class. After the kids have named all the commandments they can think of, signal the readers to continue. Close the reading at the end of verse 27. Then ask:

● **What did Jesus ask the young man to do?** (Sell everything; give money to the poor and follow him.)

● **Why did the young man go away sad?** (Because he was rich and didn't want to sell everything.)

● **What was most important to the young man?** (Keeping his riches.)

TEACHER TIP

You may want to choose readers as kids arrive and allow them to look over their parts in Mark 10:17-27 before class.

● **Do you think the young man cared about Jesus? Explain.** (Yes, because he came to Jesus and asked what to do; no, because he wouldn't do what Jesus asked.)

● **How do you think Jesus felt when the young man walked away?** (Sad; disappointed.)

Say: **The Bible tells us that ★ God deserves first place in our lives. Jesus must have been sad when the young man decided that his riches were more important than obeying and following Jesus. It's not always easy for us to put God first in our lives, either.**

LIFE APPLICATION

God Is First

Say: **Let's have some fun thinking about things we enjoy—things that are important to us.**

Distribute photocopies of the "God Is First" handout (p. 17), scissors, and markers or crayons. Form groups of four. Make sure there's at least one reader in each group who can help nonreaders understand how to complete the handout. Circulate among the groups and offer help to any who need it.

Have kids cut out the completed quilt squares and share what they wrote or drew with the other members of their groups. Then gather everyone together and ask:

● **What new things did you learn about the people in your group?** (Stacey does gymnastics; Jon likes to read.)

Say: **It looks like we have some really interesting people in this class! I'm glad to see that you're involved in so many wonderful things.**

COMMITMENT

Hidden Cross

Say: **Let's take a moment to read the Bible verse that's printed in the center diamond of your handout.**

Have a volunteer read Matthew 6:33 aloud. Then ask:

● **What does this verse tell you about the things you wrote or drew?** (That they're not as important as God; that those things are good, but God should be #1 in our lives.)

● **What happens when one interest or hobby or person becomes more important than loving and obeying God?** (We get in trouble; it makes God sad.)

● **What do you see in this design besides triangles**

TEACHER TIP

If your students enjoy art, encourage them to color in the small triangles. Consider preparing a colored sample before class to help kids visualize how the finished square might look. When the colored squares are assembled on the wall during the closing activity, they'll make a beautiful display.

15

and squares? Encourage kids to study the handout until someone realizes that the design makes a cross.

Say: ★ **God deserves first place in our lives. When we make loving and obeying God the most important thing we do, our lives become like a beautiful pattern, with God right in the center.**

Have kids re-form their groups of four and discuss this question:

● **What does putting God first mean to you?** (Taking time to learn about God; praying every day; obeying what the Bible says.)

Challenge kids to sign their names in the center diamond of their handouts to show their commitment to give God first place in their lives.

Say: **Now tell the members of your group one thing you'll do to give God first place in your life this week.**

After groups have shared, call kids together and encourage them to share what they learned in their group discussions.

CLOSING

Off the Wall

Invite one group of four to tape its squares together on a wall, as shown in the illustration in the margin. Then invite the other groups one by one to add their squares. Help kids arrange their squares so the completed display forms a connected design. Ask:

● **What does our completed display make you think of?** (A pretty quilt; that God puts us all together like this in our church; that we make a beautiful pattern together.)

Hold up the treasure box.

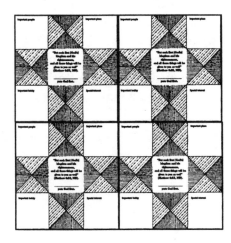

Say: **The rich young man had many beautiful things in his life. But because those things were more important to him than God, he went away sad.** Gesture toward the wall display. **We have wonderful things in our lives, too. But** ★ **God deserves first place in our lives. Jesus said that when we give God first place, God will take care of everything else. And that's a promise!**

Close class with a prayer similar to this one: **Lord, thank you for loving us and filling our lives with so many wonderful things. Please help us give you first place in our lives, and we'll trust you to take care of everything else. In Jesus' name, amen.**

16

GOD IS FIRST

What things are important to you? Write or draw the people, place, hobby, and interest that are most important to you in the four corners of the square below. You may want to color in all the small triangles. Then cut out the completed square.

Important people

Important place

"But seek first [God's] kingdom and his righteousness, and all these things will be given to you as well" (Matthew 6:33, NIV).

_____ puts God first.

Important hobby

Special interest

Circle of Forgiveness

LESSON AIM

To help kids understand that ★ God forgives us as we forgive others.

YOU'LL NEED

- ❏ two to four sets of dominoes
- ❏ two adults to play the roles of Jacob and Esau (optional)
- ❏ bathrobes, sandals, and towels for costumes
- ❏ photocopies of the "Twin Troubles" script (p. 21)
- ❏ Bibles
- ❏ pencil
- ❏ photocopies of the "Cup of Forgiveness" handout (p. 26)
- ❏ 8-inch squares of paper
- ❏ a pitcher of water

OBJECTIVES

Kids will
- ● experience frustration setting up dominoes,
- ● learn how Jacob and Esau forgave each other,
- ● understand that God wants them to accept his forgiveness and pass it on to others, and
- ● ask God's help in forgiving others.

BIBLE BASIS

Genesis 25–33

The story of Jacob and Esau is a story of grace. Sibling rivalry and parental favoritism created an ugly environment of trickery and hatred between the twin sons of Isaac. But God intervened and used these less-than-perfect heroes to perpetuate the Messianic line begun by Abraham.

After years of hatred and estrangement, the reunion of Jacob and Esau is nothing less than miraculous. Jacob had stolen Esau's two most precious possessions: the birthright and blessing of the firstborn. During their years of living apart, Esau had plenty of time to nurse his grief and hatred.

But no blood was shed, no hard words spoken. "Esau ran to meet Jacob and put his arms around him and hugged him.

18

Then Esau kissed him, and they both cried" (Genesis 33:4). What a beautiful, touching scene!

Our God is a God of grace and mercy. The mercy God shows us, he also requires of us.

1 Peter 4:8

When people intentionally hurt us, our first human reaction may be to defend ourselves. Our second reaction is almost always to think of ways to strike back.

People who know God know that the healing of a broken relationship is far more powerful and gratifying than revenge. Love is stronger than hate, and in the lives of God's people, love must always prevail.

UNDERSTANDING YOUR KIDS

"No fair!" How many times have you heard that from your students? Kids have a strong sense of justice, especially when they're the victims! And when they don't think justice is being served, their objections will come through loud and clear.

For younger children, forgiveness can be a confusing issue. When they're wronged, they want justice and they want it now. When a parent or teacher fails to exact a satisfactory punishment, they're upset. A young child often learns the best lessons about mercy and forgiveness when he or she is the wrongdoer—the one who broke the plate, hit a friend, or made the baby cry with an unkind word or action.

Older children may have entered the "grudge zone" where it's cool to run in cliques and put down their enemies. Kids in the middle grades need to be challenged to put themselves in other people's shoes and to respond in love.

That's a big order—one that many adults find difficult. But it's what God requires of us, and, in his grace, empowers us to do.

ATTENTION GRABBER

The Lesson

Knock Me Down

As kids arrive, assign them to one of two groups. Keep the balance of younger and older students the same in each group. Give both groups a set or two of dominoes and challenge them to make a design with the dominoes that will fall over when one of the dominoes is pushed.

Visit the groups as work progresses. When a group is nearly done, pretend to adjust one of the dominoes and "accidentally" knock over the entire arrangement. Apologize, then back away from the scene of the accident straight into the other group's dominoes. Apologize again, then call a halt to the work and ask:

● **What did you think when I knocked over your dominoes and ruined your hard work?** (I couldn't believe you did that; it was frustrating.)

● **How would you feel about me if I knocked over the dominoes by accident—just because I was clumsy?** (I wouldn't feel so bad; I wouldn't be mad at you.)

● **How would you feel if you knew I knocked over the dominoes on purpose and that I'd keep knocking them over again and again?** (I might cry; I'd probably get mad at you; I'd quit trying to set them up.)

● **If I said I was sorry would you still be mad at me?** (Maybe; I'm not sure; not if you never did it again.)

Say: **It can be hard to forgive people, especially if they do hurtful things on purpose, and *most* especially if they do them again and again. Today we're going to learn that ★ God forgives us as we forgive others. Later in our class we'll work with the dominoes again—and this time I promise not to knock them over! Now let's listen to a story of two brothers who had a lot to forgive.**

BIBLE STUDY

Twin Troubles (Genesis 25:27-34; 27:1-45; 32:9-21; 33:1-4)

You may want to invite two adults from your congregation to read the roles of Jacob and Esau. Simple costumes such as bathrobes, sandals, and towels wrapped with fabric strips for headgear will add to the effect when two Bible characters suddenly appear in your class to tell the Bible story.

Or, you may choose two students who are good readers to take the roles of Jacob and Esau.

In either case, assign half the students to belong to Jacob's group and the other half to belong to Esau's. Have the Jacob and Esau characters stand facing each other, with their groups behind them.

Twin Troubles

Esau: I'm Esau. My brother Jacob and I are twins, but I was the first to be born. That gave me the right to get almost all my father's money and land. My father is really proud of me because I'm a great hunter.

Jacob: I'm Jacob. One thing I can tell you about my twin brother Esau is that he's not too smart. One day he was out hunting and came back really hungry. I had just finished fixing a pot of soup. It smelled good, and Esau wanted some right away. So I said, "Sure, you can have the soup if you'll give me your rights as the firstborn son." Esau agreed. I couldn't believe it. He traded away all his rights as firstborn son for a pot of soup!

Esau: One day when my father was very old, he called me in and asked me to go hunting and prepare him a meal of delicious meat. He told me that after he had eaten the meal I prepared, he would give me his blessing—the one thing Jacob hadn't taken from me.

Jacob: So while Esau went off to hunt, my mother prepared a meal of goat meat. My father couldn't see very well, so we thought we could trick him into giving me his blessing if I pretended to be Esau. It worked! My father gave me the blessing for the oldest son before Esau got back from his hunting trip.

Esau: I hurried back from my hunting trip and prepared a tasty meal for my father. Then I took it to him, only to discover that he had just given his blessing to my scheming brother, Jacob. What a dirty trick! I decided right then that I would kill Jacob.

Jacob: My mother heard about Esau's plans to kill me, so she sent me far away to my uncle's house. Saying goodbye to my parents was hard because I didn't know if I'd ever see them again. I lived many years at my uncle's house. I got married and had a big family. But I longed to return to my old home. Still . . . Esau had threatened to kill me. And who could blame him? I cheated him out of all of his rights as firstborn son.

Esau: Many years passed. One day I looked up and saw well-dressed servants coming toward me bringing flocks of goats, sheep, camels, cows, and donkeys. They said they were from my brother, Jacob. So Jacob was on his way home. I'd wondered for a long time if I'd ever see him again.

Jacob: I prayed all night before I went to meet Esau. I asked God to protect me from Esau's anger for stealing his share of my father's possessions. You can imagine how I felt when I looked in the distance and saw Esau coming with about 400 men. I wondered if this would be the end of me.

Esau: Jacob wasn't prepared for the welcome I gave him. You can read about it in Genesis 33:4.

Say: **Our Bible story comes from the book of Genesis. It's about two brothers—twins—who didn't get along very well.**

As the characters read through the "Twin Troubles" script (p. 21), encourage the kids in both groups to cheer for their characters.

At the end of the story, hand out Bibles and have everyone look up Genesis 33:4. Be sure to pair nonreaders with older students who can find the verse and point out the words. Have a volunteer from each group read the verse aloud together with the other group's volunteer. Then have the Jacob and Esau characters shake hands or hug each other as the rest of the kids hug or shake hands with kids from the opposite group. Ask:

● **Did the ending of this story surprise you? Why or why not?** (Yes, because I expected them to fight; no, because I've heard it before.)

● **What would you have done if you'd been in Esau's shoes?** (I'd have chased Jacob away; I'd have forgiven him if he'd asked me to; I'm not sure.)

● **Why didn't Esau try to kill Jacob?** (Because God helped him forgive Jacob; because a long time had passed, and Esau realized he still loved his brother.)

● **How do you think God felt when Jacob and Esau forgave each other? Explain.** (Happy, because God loves everyone; glad that they were friends again.)

Say: **Sometimes it's hard to forgive people who do mean things to us. But the Bible tells us that ★ God forgives us as we forgive each other. Let's find out more about what that means.**

LIFE APPLICATION

No Tricks Allowed

Form three groups. Make sure you have an older student in each group.

Say: **You're going to help me make up a story. I'll take turns asking each group to give me a word for our story. When it's your group's turn, make a huddle and then call out the word you choose. I'll tell you exactly what kind of word I need. When we've filled in all the blanks, I'll read our story out loud.**

Jot down kids responses in the blanks of the "Championship Trick" story (p. 23). Then read the story aloud, inserting the kids' words as you read.

Championship Trick

It was the bottom of the ninth. The ___(town)___ Hornets and the ___(another town)___ Stingers were in a fight for the ___(name of animal)___ league championship. The game had been really ___(adjective)___, and everyone was feeling ___(adjective)___. ___(boy's name)___ stepped up to bat. The crowd grew even more ___(adjective)___. The Hornets fans were yelling, "___(verb)___, Hornets, ___(same verb)___." The Stingers fans were yelling, "___(verb)___, Stingers, ___(same verb)___." ___(same boy)___ ___(past tense of verb)___ the bat and stared ___(adverb)___ at the pitcher. Two men on, two outs. This was it—the championship.

The pitch ___(past tense of verb)___ in. ___(same boy)___ swung. The bat hit the ball with a loud ___(sound)___. The ball ___(past tense of verb)___ into center field—a base hit! ___(same boy)___ ___(past tense of verb)___ down the line toward first base. But suddenly he ___(past tense of verb)___ to the ground with a thud. While ___(same boy)___ was at bat, the catcher had untied both his shoelaces, causing him to trip. The ___(adjective)___ center fielder threw the ball to the first baseman well before ___(same boy)___ arrived. The game was over—ended on a ___(adjective)___ trick.

Read the story aloud and enjoy a good laugh. Then say: **That's pretty funny, but when someone hurts you or plays a trick on you in real life, it's not funny at all. In fact, you may feel like doing something to get back at that person. But let's read about what God wants us to do.**

Have a volunteer read 1 Peter 4:8. Then have another volunteer summarize the verse in his or her own words.

Say: **In your groups, tell about a time you were able to forgive someone and how it felt to do that. Let's have two rules: Don't use people's real names and don't tell about anyone in this room.**

Travel from group to group as kids share. After two or

three minutes, say: **Now let's do something fun that shows us how God's forgiveness works.**

COMMITMENT

Cup of Forgiveness

Distribute photocopies of the "Cup of Forgiveness" handout (p. 26) and 8-inch squares of paper. Have everyone watch as you demonstrate how to fold the cup. Then have kids work together in their groups as they each fold their own cups. Encourage kids who are quick with their paper folding to help others complete their cups.

Then form one large circle. Pour water from a pitcher into your cup as you say: **Forgiveness comes from God. ★ God forgives us as we forgive others.** As you say "others," pour the water from your cup into the cup of the student on your right. Have that student repeat the sentence "God forgives us as we forgive others," and pour the water into the next student's cup. Continue in that manner around the circle.

If someone spills the water, refill his or her cup from the pitcher and say: **God's forgiveness never runs dry.** Then continue until the water comes back to you.

Say: **God's forgiveness works just like our circle. We receive forgiveness from God, then we pass that forgiveness on to others. Our circle of forgiveness becomes a circle of love. Hold your cup in both hands and think of one person you need to forgive. Silently pray and ask God to help you love and forgive that person.**

After a few moments of silence, pray: **Thank you, Lord, for your gift of forgiveness. Help us pass that gift on to others. In Jesus' name, amen.**

CLOSING

Circle of Love

Say: **Remember my promise that we'd do something more with the dominoes? Now is the time! Let's make one big circle using all the dominoes and see if we can all get inside the circle without knocking them down.**

24

Have everyone step inside the completed circle. Ask:

● **What did we learn today?** (God forgives us as we for-give others).

Say: **Let's shout that aloud together, then** (name the youngest child) **can push the first domino in our circle of love.**

Encourage kids to keep their cups as reminders of God's forgiveness.

CUP OF FORGIVENESS

"Love each other deeply, because love will cause many sins to be forgiven" (1 Peter 4:8).

1. Fold a square of paper in half, forming a triangle that points upward.

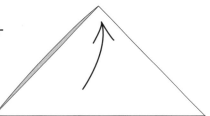

2. Fold the bottom right corner to the top left edge.

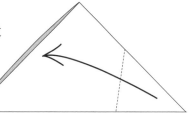

3. Turn the paper over. Fold the bottom right corner to the top left edge.

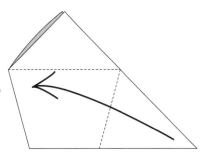

5. Here's your finished cup!

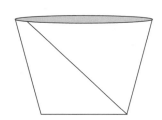

4. Fold the top front flap into the front pocket. Fold the back flap into the back pocket.

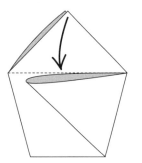

The Trust Test

3

LESSON AIM

To help kids understand that ★ God will always take care of us.

OBJECTIVES

Kids will
- catch unknown objects while blindfolded,
- learn how Jesus helped in Peter's moment of need,
- identify life events that are scary, and
- make a commitment to trust God during life's storms.

BIBLE BASIS

Matthew 14:22-33

After feeding the 5,000, Jesus ordered his disciples to get into a boat and cross the Sea of Galilee. Then he went up into the hills to pray. Sometime in the wee hours of the night, a fierce storm struck the disciples' boat. When Jesus came to them, walking on the water, the disciples were frightened, fearing he was a ghost. Immediately Jesus reassured them, saying, "Have courage! It is I. Do not be afraid."

Peter jumped at the chance to do something extraordinary: He asked permission to walk to Jesus on the water. Jesus said, "Come." The venture began successfully, but soon the wind and waves distracted Peter, and he began to sink. Matthew's description of Jesus' reaction is one of the most beautiful lines in Scripture. "Immediately Jesus reached out

YOU'LL NEED

- ❏ blindfolds
- ❏ soft foam balls
- ❏ small pillows
- ❏ marshmallows
- ❏ rolled-up newspapers
- ❏ coins
- ❏ a mop or broom
- ❏ a spray bottle filled with water
- ❏ photocopies of the "In God's Hands" handout (p. 34)
- ❏ scissors

his hand and caught Peter."

Jesus will always come to us in the storms of life. He offers his loving hand and catches us before the wind and waves completely overwhelm us. Peter began to sink but didn't drown because he trusted the one who offered to save him.

John 14:1

Chapters 13–17 of John paint an intimate picture of Jesus' interaction with his disciples just before his arrest and crucifixion. In this passage, Jesus prepares his followers for the trauma ahead. Listen carefully to what he says: "Don't let your hearts be troubled. Trust in God, and trust in me."

Choice is clearly implied. We can let ourselves be troubled, or we can choose to trust.

UNDERSTANDING YOUR KIDS

Because of the mixed messages kids hear, it's difficult for them to know where to put their trust. Humanistic thinkers say, "You can do anything you set your mind to," which is really another way of saying, "Trust in yourself." Gangs have great appeal to kids. Their message is "Trust in the group—we'll take care of everything." You'd like to tell your students that they can always trust in their parents and friends, but that's not always the case because there's no such thing as a perfect parent or a perfect friend. But Jesus is a friend who never fails. He is all-knowing, all-loving, and all-powerful.

As much as you'd like to protect your students, they will be battered by life's storms. Some will be caught in divorce; some will move and lose their base of friends; some will experience learning disabilities; some will face hostile cliques at school. How wonderful to be able to reassure kids that Jesus will always be there, always ready to stretch his hand through the storm and bring them safely through.

The Lesson ATTENTION GRABBER

Coming Your Way

Help kids form pairs. It's a good idea to pair older children with younger ones. Distribute blindfolds and have one partner in each pair blindfold the other. Have each seeing partner guide his or her blindfolded partner to stand against a wall of the classroom. Then ask the seeing partners to stand five or six feet away.

Put a pile of tossable objects on the floor near the seeing partners. Include items such as soft foam balls, small pillows, marshmallows, rolled-up newspapers, and coins.

Say: **We're going to play a game called Coming Your Way. Here's how it works. Partners who can see will choose any of the items in this pile on the floor to toss very gently to their blindfolded partners. They won't give any clues about what they're tossing. Just before they toss, they'll say, "Coming your way!" and their partner's name. Toss carefully—you want your partner to catch as many items as possible. Ready? Go!**

After each toss, have the seeing partners retrieve the items and place them in the pile for other students to toss. After four or five tosses, have partners change roles. After four or five more tosses, call time. Have kids place all the items and the blindfolds in a corner of the room where they won't be a distraction. Then call everyone together and ask:

● **Who was able to catch one item? two items? three items? four items?**

● **What was it like to try to catch something that you couldn't see?** (Scary; hard; fun.)

● **What would've made it easier?** (Being able to see; knowing what was coming.)

● **How was this game like what happens in real life when problems and scary things come our way?** (We can't see what's coming; we never know what's going to happen.)

● **When you were the tosser, what did you do to help your blindfolded partner?** (Tried to warn her; tossed carefully so he could catch it.)

● **How is that like what Jesus does for us when scary things come our way?** (Jesus takes care of us; Jesus tries to help us.)

Say: **Today we're going to learn that ★ God will always take care of us. Let's see how Jesus took care of his disciples in a really scary situation.**

TEACHER TIP

Let the size of your class determine how many students you appoint to be disciples and parts of the boat. If you have a very large class, you might want to have several kids be waves that surround the boat.

The Water Walker (Matthew 14:22-33)

Say: **The first thing we need to do is get in position for our Bible story. First, I need some people to be disciples and sit close together in the middle of the floor.** Select a few students and place them together as if they are in a boat. Then hold up a mop or broom, handle down. **This represents Peter. You disciples hold up Peter right here in the center of the boat. Good.**

Now I need people to be the boat. Let's make the pointed ends of the boat be here and here. Put children in position at the points. **Now the rest of the boat people join hands and surround Peter and the disciples. Great! Now we're ready for the story. This story took place right after Jesus fed more than 5,000 people with five loaves of bread and two fish. Jesus and his disciples were tired, and they wanted to rest. Listen carefully and act out what happens as I tell this story from Matthew 14:22-33.**

As you read the Bible passage, pause to coach students with appropriate actions.

Jesus told his followers to get into the boat and go ahead of him across the lake. He stayed there to send the people home. Have the disciples and the boat rock gently as the journey across the lake begins. **After he had sent them away, he went by himself up into the hills to pray. It was late, and Jesus was there alone. By this time, the boat was already far away from land.** Have the disciples shield their eyes and peer into the distance. **It was being hit by waves, because the wind was blowing against it.** Have everyone rock from side to side in unison as the boat lurches in the storm. Gently squirt the students with water from a spray bottle.

Between 3 and 6 o'clock in the morning, Jesus came to them, walking on the water. Have the disciples peer into the distance. **When his followers saw him walking on the water, they were afraid. They said, "It's a ghost!" and cried out in fear.** Have the disciples gasp.

But Jesus quickly spoke to them, "Have courage! It is I. Do not be afraid." Have the disciples give a deep sigh of relief.

Peter said, "Lord, if it is really you, then command me to come to you on the water."

Jesus said, "Come."

Peter left the boat and walked on the water to Jesus.

Have the disciples and boat people move the mop toward you. Remind everyone to keep rocking with the storm. **But when Peter saw the wind and the waves, he became afraid and began to sink.** Have the person holding the mop let it tilt over. **He shouted, "Lord, save me!"** Have the person holding the mop bounce it up and down.

Immediately Jesus reached out his hand and caught Peter. Pick up the mop. **Jesus said, "Your faith is small. Why did you doubt?"**

After they got into the boat, the wind became calm. Pass the mop back into the boat. Have everyone stop rocking. **Then those who were in the boat worshiped Jesus and said, "Truly you are the Son of God!"** Have all the disciples and the mop bow.

Have kids give themselves a round of applause and gather in a circle. Ask:

● **What's surprising to you about this story?** (That Jesus could walk on the water; that Peter wanted to get out of the boat.)

● **Why do you think Peter wanted to walk on the water to Jesus?** (Because he was a showoff; because he wanted to see if he could do it; because he knew Jesus would save him if he got in trouble.)

● **Why do you think Peter started to sink?** (Because he got scared; because he looked at the storm instead of looking at Jesus.)

● **How did the disciples feel about Jesus when he saved Peter and calmed the storm?** (They wanted to worship him; they knew he was God's Son.)

● **How do you feel about Jesus after hearing this story?** (I'm glad he's my friend; I believe Jesus can do anything; I'm not sure what I think.)

Say: **Peter knew he could count on Jesus' help. We can trust Jesus, too. When we face scary things in our lives, it's important to remember that ★ God will always take care of us.**

LIFE APPLICATION

Waves

Say: **The wind and the waves frightened the disciples in our story. Now we're going to make some waves of our own and tell about things that frighten us.**

Arrange chairs in a circle.

Say: **I'm going to start by telling about a really scary thing that happened to me and how God took care of me. Then I'll start a wave by standing up, throwing my arms up in the air, then sitting down. The next person will stand up, then the next person, and so on 'til the wave comes all the way back to me. Then** (name of person on your left) **will tell about a scary situation and how God took care of** (him or her) **and start another wave.**

Begin with your own story and have kids share their stories around the circle, with a wave after each story. If kids are unsure about what to share, invite them to tell about something they were scared about when they were really little.

Then say: ★ **God will always take care of us. We'll have storms in our lives, that's for sure. And we may not know when they're coming or what they'll be. But when we see how God has taken care of us in the past and how he's taken care of all our friends, we can trust him to take care of us in the future.**

COMMITMENT

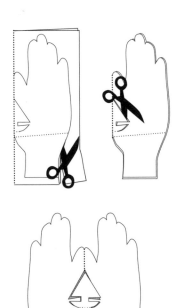

Scare Shares

Have kids find their partners from the opening activity. Distribute scissors and photocopies of the "In God's Hands" handout (p. 34). Show kids how to cut and fold the handout to create a paper sculpture of hands holding a sailboat. It's helpful to a have a finished model of the paper sculpture so kids can see how it works. Remind older kids to help their young partners who may have difficulty cutting and folding the sculpture.

Say: **After you've finished your paper sculpture, sit knee to knee with your partner and tell about a scary situation you're facing now or may face in the future. You might tell about a class in school that's hard for you, about a bully in your neighborhood, or about a big ballgame that's coming up.**

After you've both shared, tell how you'll trust God in those scary situations. Then shake hands and say, ★ **"God will always take care of you."**

In God's Hands

After partners have shared, have everyone stand in a circle, linking elbows and holding the paper sculptures. Rock the circle from side to side a bit and say: **We've all talked about scary things we're facing right now or that we'll face in the future. Talking about those things can make us feel a little unsteady.** Stop the rocking motion. **The good news is that ★ God will always take care of us. Let's read together the words of Jesus printed on our paper sculptures.**

Read the verse more than once so that nonreaders have a chance to learn to "read" it. Then close in prayer.

Pray: **Lord Jesus, thank you for the way you rescued Peter and calmed the storm. Help us to trust you to be with us in the storms we face in our lives. We put ourselves in your hands. In Jesus' name, amen.**

IN GOD'S HANDS

Fold on the dotted center line, then cut on the solid lines. Fold on the bottom dotted line, overlap the bottom pieces, and tape or staple them together to make the sculpture stand up.

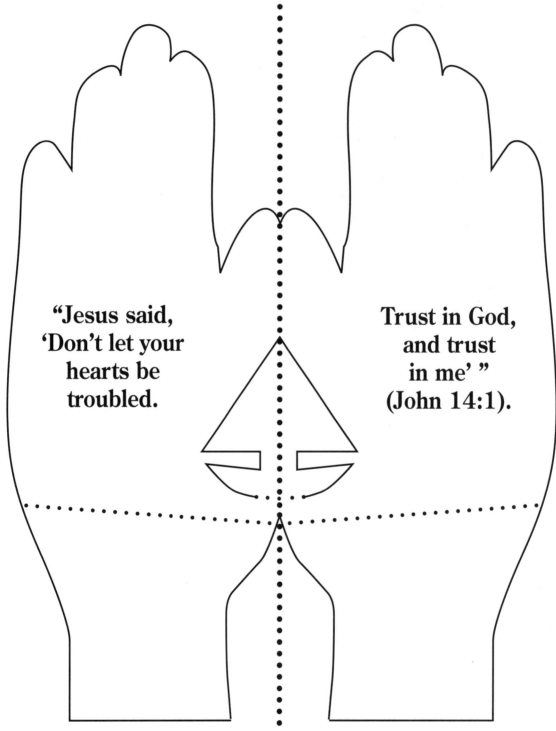

"Jesus said, 'Don't let your hearts be troubled.

Trust in God, and trust in me' " (John 14:1).

More Like Jesus

4

LESSON AIM

To help kids see that ★ Jesus wants us to be like him.

OBJECTIVES

Kids will
● reproduce their partners' drawings without seeing them;
● learn how Peter failed, then grew in faith;
● experience "circuit training" in ways to mature in faith; and
● make a commitment to be more like Jesus.

YOU'LL NEED

❑ pencils
❑ paper
❑ a cassette tape of the Bible story and a cassette player (optional)
❑ photocopies of the "Cross Training" handout (p. 42)
❑ scissors
❑ glue sticks or tape
❑ a whistle (optional)
❑ a Bible

BIBLE BASIS

Luke 22:31-34, 54-62

These passages present the poignant story of Peter's intention to be loyal to Jesus even to the point of death, and his miserable failure to carry out those intentions.

Jesus knew Peter's shortcomings and twice prophesied clearly about Satan's imminent attack and Peter's failure. In between the negative prophecies, Jesus offered Peter the reassurance that because of Jesus' own prayers, Peter wouldn't completely fail. And Jesus encouraged Peter to be strong and help the other disciples when Peter returned from his self-imposed exile.

Jesus saw all Peter's shortcomings—and his potential. He showed deep compassion and love for Peter by forgiving him and gently restoring him before the acts of denial even took place.

Acts 3:1-10; 4:1-20

Can this healer and fearless spokesman for Christ be the same coward who denied his Lord three times? What a transformation! How wonderfully encouraging to see what the power of God can do with a far-from-perfect person.

UNDERSTANDING YOUR KIDS

Peter is a hero kids can identify with. He's the first one to speak and the last one to think. He overestimates his abilities. He flounders in the waves. He makes big promises he can't keep. He desperately wants to succeed but often falls short.

Kids experience all these feelings. They want to be grown up. They want to show they're responsible and make their own decisions. But good intentions often end in disappointment or failure. Maturity doesn't happen overnight—it comes through painful struggles similar to the ones Peter experienced. This lesson will help you show your kids that God's love for them is greater than any failure could ever be.

Peter's grand flops are followed by grander miracles. God completely transforms Peter's character and makes him a key leader of the church in Jerusalem. Kids need to see that God can do the same with them. With God in charge of their lives, each embarrassment or failure can become a steppingstone to being more like Christ.

The Lesson   ATTENTION GRABBER

Partner Pictures

Distribute pencils and paper. Have kids find partners and sit back to back.

Say: **The younger partner in your pair will draw a simple picture of anything—flowers, a house, trees, or mountains. As the younger partner draws, he or she will explain each step of the drawing without saying what the drawing is. The older partner will listen and try to draw the same picture. You'll have about two minutes. Ready? Start drawing.**

Call time after two minutes. Have partners take turns showing their pairs of pictures to the class. Give everyone a round of applause for their good efforts. Then ask:

● **What did you think when you first compared your picture to your partner's picture?** (I didn't think they looked the same at all; they looked sort of the same.)

● **What was it like trying to match your partner's picture without being able to see it?** (Frustrating; kind of fun.)

● **What was it like trying to explain what you were drawing?** (I couldn't explain it very well; I didn't know how to tell exactly what I was drawing.)

● **What could we change to make this activity easier?** (We could draw side by side instead of back to back so that both partners could see each other's drawing.)

Say: **Let's try it again. I'll give you each another sheet of paper. This time, sit side by side. The older partner gets to draw this time, and the younger partner will copy the drawing. You've got two more minutes. Go!**

Call time after two minutes. Then have partners lay both sets of drawings in front of them. Ask:

● **Why does the second set of drawings match so much better?** (Because we could see what our partners were drawing.)

Say: **Did you know that's one reason Jesus came to earth? Listen while I explain. God wanted people to be loving, just as God is loving. So God told Moses and other Old Testament prophets how he wanted people to live. But that was hard for people—just like drawing a picture from your partner's instructions was hard.**

Then Jesus came to earth to *show* us how to live. Jesus was an example we could see and understand, just as you could see your partner's drawing when you sat side by side. ★ Jesus wants us to be like him. Today we're going to talk about how we can be like Jesus.

TEACHER TIP

As kids are drawing, wander around and give encouragement. You may want to help younger children give oral instructions to their partners.

BIBLE STUDY

The Problem With Peter (Luke 22:31-34, 54-62; Acts 3:1-10; 4:1-20)

Say: **Our Bible story today is about one of Jesus' closest friends. Jesus had twelve disciples, but three were especially close friends—Peter, James, and John. Jesus took those three friends with him sometimes when he left the rest of the disciples behind. So you'd think that Peter would truly understand how to be like Jesus.**

Well, sometimes Peter did really well, and sometimes he fell flat on his face. Today we're going to get to know Peter better by taking a peek into what his diary might have been like. Ask:

● **How many of you keep a diary? What kinds of things do you write in it?** (Things that happen to me; what I do with my friends; what I pray about.)

Say: **Let's listen to what Peter might have written in his diary during the week of Jesus' death and resurrection.**

Read aloud the "Friday Evening" section of "Peter's Diary," then pause and ask:

● **Based on the story you just heard, what words would you use to describe Peter?** (A failure; a coward; he brags; he doesn't keep his promises; he disappoints his friends.)

● **How do you think Jesus felt about Peter at this point?** (Jesus still loved him; Jesus was disappointed in him; he hurt Jesus' feelings; Jesus cared about him and prayed for him.)

● **If you had been in Peter's shoes, what would you have done when the soldiers and priests came to arrest Jesus?** (I would have run away; I would have tried to fight.)

● **Who can tell about a time when you felt like Peter must have felt after he said he didn't know Jesus?** (When I broke my mom's favorite vase; when I told on one of my friends to get back at him.)

Say: **All of us have times when we fall flat on our faces. We're not perfect. But God loves us anyway. Sometimes God even uses our failures to teach us how to be more like Jesus. Let's listen to the section of Peter's imaginary diary titled "Two Months Later."**

Read aloud the last segment of the Bible story, then ask:

● **What words would you use to describe Peter now?** (Strong; brave; a miracle worker; like Jesus.)

● **Why is this Peter so much different?** (Jesus forgave him; God's Holy Spirit helped him; he had more faith because Jesus rose from the dead.)

Say: **The wonderful thing about God is that he never gives up on us. When we give our lives to God, we can trust God to make us more and more like Jesus. That doesn't mean we'll be perfect, but it does mean we'll get better all the time. And that makes Jesus happy because ★ Jesus wants us to be like him.**

Peter's Diary

Friday Evening

The last 24 hours have been the most terrible of my whole life. I'm so confused. It started when we ate the Passover meal with Jesus. He was quiet and sad. He told us that he would soon suffer and go away from us. Then he told me that I would be tested and that he had prayed that I wouldn't lose my faith.

I said, "Jesus, I would go to prison with you and even die with you." But Jesus answered, "Before the rooster crows, you'll say three times that you don't know me."

I couldn't believe it. I would never do anything like that—at least I didn't think I would.

After dinner we left the city and went out to the Mount of Olives. Jesus went off to pray and asked us to pray with him. But we all fell asleep.

Then, before we knew it, Jesus was waking us up. Soldiers and priests came and arrested Jesus. I grabbed my sword and cut off the ear of one of the servants. But Jesus told me to put my sword away. Then he healed the servant's ear.

As they led Jesus away, we all scattered. I followed Jesus at a distance. They took him to the house of the high priest. Soldiers started a fire in the middle of the courtyard. I stood near the fire to keep warm. I could see what they were doing to Jesus—it was awful. They beat him and made fun of him. I didn't know what to do.

A servant girl pointed to me and said, "This man was with Jesus."

"I don't even know him," I replied.

Then another person said, "You're one of his disciples."

"No, I'm not!" I replied. I was afraid that the soldiers would arrest me, too.

About an hour later, another man said, "You were with Jesus—you're from Galilee."

"I don't know what you're talking about!" I shouted.

Just then a rooster crowed. Jesus turned his head and looked at me. His eyes were so sad. I ran away into the darkness and cried for the rest of the night.

Today they crucified him. Jesus is dead. My life is in pieces.

Two Months Later

So much has happened since that terrible Friday when Jesus died. He rose again on Sunday and appeared to us several times. He forgave me for denying him and asked me to help take care of his people.

Then one day as we were talking together on a mountaintop, Jesus rose into the sky. Angels told us Jesus would come again someday.

We went back to Jerusalem to pray for the Holy Spirit Jesus had promised. As we were praying together, the Holy Spirit filled the room. We went out and started preaching to the people in Jerusalem. Many people believed.

One day John and I went to the temple to pray. A man who couldn't walk asked us for money. I said to the man, "I don't have any silver or gold, but I do have something else I can give you. By the power of Jesus Christ from Nazareth, stand up and walk!" And he did.

That attracted a big crowd of people, so I told them about Jesus. The priests got really angry—the same priests who had Jesus killed. So they dragged us off to court and told us not to preach about Jesus anymore.

But we said, "Should we obey you or God? We cannot keep quiet. We must speak about what we have seen and heard."

LIFE APPLICATION

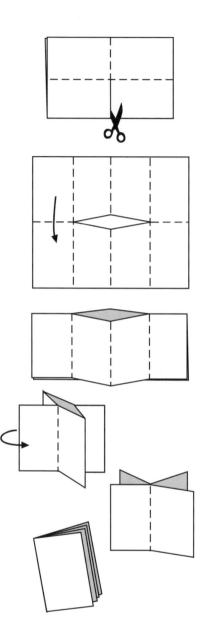

Cross Training

Say: **Let's have some fun finding out how we can be more like Jesus. Can anyone explain what cross training is? In cross training you do some exercises to make your heart and lungs healthy and other exercises to strengthen your muscles. Today we're going to do a different kind of cross training. Our cross training will show us how to be more like Jesus. We'll have four different stations. At each station you'll learn one way to be more like Jesus.**

Distribute photocopies of the "Cross Training" handout (p. 42), scissors, and glue sticks or tape. Demonstrate how to fold on the dotted lines and cut on the solid lines. Then show kids how to hold the paper the long way, grasp the ends, and push them together. The sections around the slit will push outward to form an eight-page booklet. Glue or tape the top and bottom center so the booklet will stand. Ask:

● **When you look at our stand-up booklet from the top, what do you see?** (A cross.)

Say: **Let's see what this cross-training booklet teaches us about how to be like Jesus.**

If you have a fairly small class with limited space, you may want to work through the four steps of the cross-training booklet as a whole group.

If you have a large group and plenty of space, consider forming four groups and setting up four stations. Place a Bible at Station 1. Appoint a leader from each group to read and direct the activity at each station. Blow a whistle every two or three minutes and have groups rotate clockwise to the next station.

After kids have worked through all four stations, gather everyone and say: **Good work! Learning to be like Jesus can be fun.**

COMMITMENT

Training Time

Help kids form pairs.

Say: **Look at the four panels of the cross-training booklet with your partner. Tell your partner when you'll do each of the things in the booklet this week. Then shake hands to show that you'll carry out your cross-training plan this week.**

40

Cross Prayer

Have kids stand in two intersecting lines, forming the shape of a cross. Close in a prayer similar to this one: **Dear Jesus, thank you for being our example. Thank you for being patient with us just as you were patient with Peter. Please help us be more like you every day. Amen.**

CROSS +RAINING

Station 4

When you make a decision, ask, "What would Jesus do?" Keep a journal (in words, pictures, or both) that tells about times you tried to do what Jesus would do. If you're facing a difficult decision, ask others to pray about it with you.

Station 1

Read (or have someone read to you) stories of Jesus' life from Matthew, Mark, Luke, or John. After you read each story, ask yourself these questions:

● What is Jesus like in this story?
● What can I do to be like Jesus?

Start with the story in Mark 10:13-16.

Station 3

Take time to encourage your friends and family. Talk about how you're growing in your faith and becoming more like Jesus. Finish sentences like these:

● (Name of person), I see Jesus in you when....
● I thank Jesus for you because....

Station 2

Talk to Jesus every day in prayer. On some days, pray this prayer that Jesus taught his disciples:

"'Our Father in heaven, hallowed be your name, your kingdom come, your will be done on earth as it is in heaven.

Give us today our daily bread. Forgive us our debts, as we also have forgiven our debtors.

And lead us not into temptation, but deliver us from the evil one'" (Matthew 6:9-13, NIV).

Showing God's Love

Promises to Keep

LESSON AIM

To help kids understand that ★ God keeps his promises, and we should, too.

OBJECTIVES

Kids will
- decide whether to believe certain promises,
- discover how God was faithful to Noah,
- learn how to make promises they can keep, and
- discover special promises from the Bible.

BIBLE BASIS

Genesis 6:9–9:17

If you were to ask the kids in your church to name their favorite Bible story, chances are good that the story of Noah and the ark would be among the top vote-getters. Why? There's an exciting, colorful plot, a huge "natural disaster," survivors watched over by a caring God, and a rainbow to top it all off! Even Hollywood's brightest imaginations and most fantastic special effects can't top this one.

What makes it even better is that "this ain't no story"! It's history, or "his-story"—God's story. It's a reliable record of what God actually did on this planet.

Despite the destruction caused by the flood, this isn't an account of vengeance—it's a story of love and promises kept. After the water recedes, God promises never again to destroy all life on earth with a flood. The rainbow seals the covenant and serves as an everlasting reminder of that promise.

YOU'LL NEED

- ❏ a 3×5 card
- ❏ scissors
- ❏ a bag of unshelled peanuts
- ❏ a stapler or tape
- ❏ markers
- ❏ photocopies of the "Promise Dove" handout (p. 52)
- ❏ 6-inch strips of ribbon in rainbow colors
- ❏ cellophane tape
- ❏ glue sticks
- ❏ a hole punch (optional)

45

But there's another significant series of promises given, acted on, and kept as the story opens. God predicts the flood, then instructs Noah to build the boat for his family and the animals. God promises that Noah and his family will enter the ark. At this point, Noah doesn't understand the full implications of this promise. But he trusts the promise maker and obeys.

Use this lesson to teach children that God keeps his promises faithfully, and we should, too.

Isaiah 40:8
In a world of confusing messages and rapid change, it's important for kids to know that they can count on God's Word. God keeps his promises today, just as he did in Noah's time.

UNDERSTANDING YOUR KIDS

What child wouldn't want to spend a few months in a floating zoo? Kids have a wonderful, God-given fascination with the diversity of God's animal creation. And that's great. But it's important not to let the natural kid-appeal of this Bible story overshadow its all-important theme: God keeps his promises.

God asked Noah to do a pretty outrageous thing. We assume that Noah's ark-building binge brought more than a few snickers from his neighbors. But God had made a covenant with Noah. A covenant is a two-way street, and Noah was determined to keep his end of the bargain.

Sometimes Christian kids who live in a secular society feel that God asks them to do some pretty hard things, too. Like returning good for evil. Walking away when test or homework answers are illicitly offered. Loving their enemies. And being faithful to their promises.

Trust, obedience, faithfulness—challenge your kids to be the Noahs of their day!

The Lesson ATTENTION GRABBER

Would Ya Believe Me?
Before class, practice cutting a 3×5 card as shown on page 47. Cutting it in this manner will allow the card to stretch

46

over a person's head. You'll also need to hide a bag of unshelled peanuts. Staple or tape the bag shut.

As kids arrive, ask:

● **Would you believe me if I promised to give you a treat that's never been touched by human hands? How many would believe a promise like that?**

Invite the kids who believed you to search the room until they find the bag. Have the person who finds the bag bring it to you. Before you open it, ask:

● **Now how many people believe my promise that this bag contains a treat that has never been touched by human hands?** Have a child who believes you open the bag. Then toss handfuls of peanuts around the class. Ask a younger student to bring his or her peanuts to the front of the class. Help the student open the peanut. Ask:

● **Who put that peanut in there?** (God did; the plant did.)

● **Has any person touched these little peanuts before?** (No.) **Are you sure?** (Yes.)

● **Then did I keep my promise?** (Yes.)

Say: **Good! You ought to be able to trust the promises made by your teacher at church.**

Give children a few moments to shell and eat their peanuts and throw away the shells. Then choose a volunteer to come to the front of the room. Show that child your 3×5 card and ask:

● **Would you believe me if I promised to make this card go over your head and around your neck?** (Yes, I trust you; no, that's impossible.)

If the child doesn't respond positively, keep asking until you find someone who believes your promise. Then bring out the scissors and cut the card as shown in the margin. Slip the cut-and-stretched card over the head of the child who believed your promise. Thank your volunteer and have him or her sit down. Then ask:

● **When I first made these promises, how many of you believed me 100 percent? Why?** (Because we know you; because we thought there was a trick to it.)

● **Those of you who didn't believe me, why didn't you believe in my promise?** (Because it sounded too strange; I didn't really think you could do that.)

● **When you saw that I kept my first promise, did that make it easier for you to believe my second promise? Why or why not?** (Yes, because you already did one thing that sounded hard, so I believed you could do another; no, because it still seemed impossible to make a small card go around somebody's head.)

1. Fold the card in half lengthwise.
2. Cut as shown, making the first cut from the folded side, the next cut from the outside, and so on.
3. When you've made all the cuts, cut through the middle fold of all but the end strips.
4. Stretch the card open into a circle.

47

● **So when people make promises, how do you decide whether or not to believe them?** (I believe them if they've kept their promises before; it depends on their reputations.)

Say: **Today we're going to talk about the fact that ★ God keeps his promises, and we should, too.**

BIBLE STUDY

Off the Deep End (Genesis 6:9–9:17)

Say: **Our Bible story today is a pretty familiar one, so we're going to approach it differently than you've probably done before. It's about one of the most famous promises in the Bible. Does anyone care to guess what it might be?**

If no one guesses, say it has something to do with colors. If you need to give another hint, say it has something to do with colors in the sky. Then challenge kids to tell you what promise the rainbow reminds them of. If no one responds, encourage kids to listen carefully to the story to find out.

Say: **OK, let's get started with the story of Noah. Here's what you need to do.**

Practice these cues and responses with the kids:

● **Whenever I say "God," fold your hands and bow.**

● **Whenever I say "neighbors," cover your mouth and laugh.**

● **Whenever I say "animals," make your favorite animal sound.**

Say: **One last thing. When I pull my finger across my throat, that means to cut off all noise immediately. Ready?**

Read aloud "Off the Deep End" (p. 49). Pause after each underlined word to let children respond to the cues.

Have kids give themselves a round of applause for their participation in the story. Then ask:

● **Why do you think Noah obeyed God and built the ark?** (Because he trusted what God said; because he wanted to make God happy.)

● **Why do you think Noah kept building even when his neighbors made fun of him?** (Because he trusted God more than he trusted his neighbors; because it's more important to please God than to please anyone else.)

● **What promises did God keep in this story?** (The promise that the flood would come; the promise to keep

TEACHER TIP

In the middle of the story, you'll find directions to have kids form three groups and do a series of sound effects that create quite a realistic storm. The larger the group, the more effective the progressive effect as groups move from one sound to the next. If your class is small, you may want to use only two groups. Let one group do a sound effect for about five seconds before the next group joins in.

48

Off the Deep End

One day <u>God</u> looked sadly upon the beautiful earth he'd made. Then <u>God</u> spoke to Noah.

"Noah, people have ruined my beautiful earth. It's full of violence and bad things. I've decided to destroy the earth and everything in it. But I want you to build an ark for yourself and your family and two of every kind of <u>animal</u>. I will send a flood, and everything on the earth will die. But I promise that you and your family and the animals will be safe in the ark."

So Noah did just as God said. He began to build a boat—a huge boat—a monstrously massive and marvelous boat. The <u>neighbors</u> couldn't quite believe their eyes.

"Check out old Noah," the <u>neighbors</u> snickered. "He's really gone off the deep end now. What's he waiting for—a flood?" Then they laughed so hard they fell over. But Noah went right on building.

The next day the <u>neighbors</u> asked, "Whatcha gonna put in that incredible crate you're building?"

"<u>Animals</u>," Noah replied.

"What kinds of <u>animals</u>?" the <u>neighbors</u> asked.

"Every kind," Noah replied.

Once again the <u>neighbors</u> laughed until they fell over.

A few weeks later Noah and his family had nearly finished the ark. They started loading hay and grain and fruit inside.

"Hey!" the <u>neighbors</u> called out. "Whatcha puttin' in there now?"

"Food," Noah replied.

"For who?" the <u>neighbors</u> asked.

"For my family and the <u>animals</u>," Noah responded.

"What if the <u>animals</u> decide to eat your family?" the <u>neighbors</u> asked. They thought their question was so funny that they fell over laughing again.

When the ark was finished, <u>God</u> sent the <u>animals</u> to Noah, who began loading them in, two by two. The <u>neighbors</u> had never seen anything quite like this. They laughed a little bit, then scratched their heads.

When little raindrops started to fall, Noah's family went into the ark, and <u>God</u> shut the door. The <u>neigh-bors</u> looked at the ark all loaded and closed up. And they looked at the dark clouds rolling across the sky. Then the rain came harder and faster, so they ran for shelter. They weren't laughing anymore.

Let's make our own rainstorm to see what it was like when the water rose and covered the whole earth. We'll start by forming three groups. (Indicate where groups one, two, and three will be divided.) When I look at your group, start doing what I'm doing. Keep doing the same thing until I look at your group and change the action.

(Look at group one and rub your hands together. Then proceed to group two, and finally to group three. Come back to group one and snap your fingers quickly. After a few seconds give the same cue to group two, then to group three.

Continue in this manner. The third cue is patting your legs lightly, and the fourth is stomping your feet.

Have the storm decrease by working backward through the cues. Have groups return to patting their legs, then snapping their fingers, then rubbing their hands together. Finally, cut the groups off one by one by pulling a finger across your throat.)

Finally the rain stopped. All the people and <u>animals</u> in the ark were safe and well. Then one day the ark bumped into the top of a mountain. The water was starting to go down.

Noah sent a raven and then a dove out of the ark. But the dove came back because there was no place to land. A week later Noah sent the dove out again. This time it came back with a leaf in its mouth. Seven days later Noah sent the dove out again. This time it didn't come back, for it had found a place to nest.

Then <u>God</u> told Noah to come out of the ark. So out came Noah and his family and all the animals. Noah built an altar to thank <u>God</u> for keeping his promise. Then <u>God</u> blessed Noah and his family and all the <u>ani-mals</u>. And <u>God</u> hung a shining rainbow in the sky as a promise never to destroy the world with a flood again.

everyone in the ark safe; the promise never to flood the earth again.)

● **How do you feel about people who keep their promises?** (I trust them; I respect them.)

● **Why is it important for Christians to keep their promises?** (So people will trust us; so people will respect our God.)

Say: **As Christians, we want to show people what God is like. When people learn that they can trust us, then someday they may learn to trust God. ★ God keeps his promises, and we should, too.**

LIFE APPLICATION

Pop-Up Promises

Ask:

● **Who can tell about a promise you kept?**

● **Who is willing to tell about a promise you made but didn't keep?**

Allow two or three children to respond to each question, then say: **Sometimes people who don't keep their promises fail because they make promises they can't keep. I'm going to read some promises. If you think the promise I read is a good one, pop up out of your chair. If it seems like a bad promise, stay seated and point your thumbs down. Here we go.**

Pause after each promise for kids' responses.

● **I promise to give everyone in class a million dollars.**

● **I promise to try hard to be a good teacher.**

● **I promise that you're all going to get straight A's in school next year.**

● **I promise to pray for you every day this week.**

Help kids form trios. Say: **In your trios, figure out what makes a good promise and what makes a bad promise. I'll give you a minute to talk about it. Then I'll ask one person from each group to tell what you decided.**

After a minute, call time and have kids share their answers.

Then say: **Great ideas! It's important to think before you make a promise. First you think, "Is this a promise I can really keep, or do I just wish I could keep it?" Sometimes you need to ask, "Would God be happy with this promise, or am I just making this promise to get something I want?" We need to be care-**

ful about the promises we make, because ★ God keeps his promises, and we should, too.

COMMITMENT

Promise Doves

Say: **Let's make reminders of the promise God made to Noah.** Have kids form pairs, matching older students with younger, nonreading students. Distribute scissors, markers, and photocopies of the "Promise Dove" handout (p. 52). Ask a volunteer to read aloud Isaiah 40:8 from the handout. Ask:

● **What does this promise from the Bible mean to you?** (That God keeps his promises; that God's Word is true.)

Say: **That verse is God's promise to you. On the blank side of your dove, write a promise you'd like to make to God. When you've finished writing, cut out the dove.**

If children have trouble thinking of promises they'd like to make to God, suggest ideas such as "I promise to pray every day," "I promise to give God first place in my life," or "I promise to do my best to be like Jesus."

As kids are working, distribute several 6-inch strips of ribbon in rainbow colors to each child. Demonstrate how to position the strips of ribbon inside the dove, then tape the ribbons in place. Have kids rub glue sticks along the other edge of the doves then press the two halves of the doves together.

TEACHER TIP

If you have extra time, you may punch a hole in the top of each dove and tie a strip of ribbon through the hole as a hanger.

CLOSING

Promise Prayers

Have kids stand in a circle holding their promise doves. Go around the circle and invite kids to share the promises they wrote to God.

Then close with a prayer similar to this one: **Thank you, Lord, for keeping your promises. Help us trust you the way Noah did. And help us make wise promises and keep them. In Jesus' name, amen.**

Encourage kids to hang their promise doves in a special place as a reminder that ★ God keeps his promises, and we should, too.

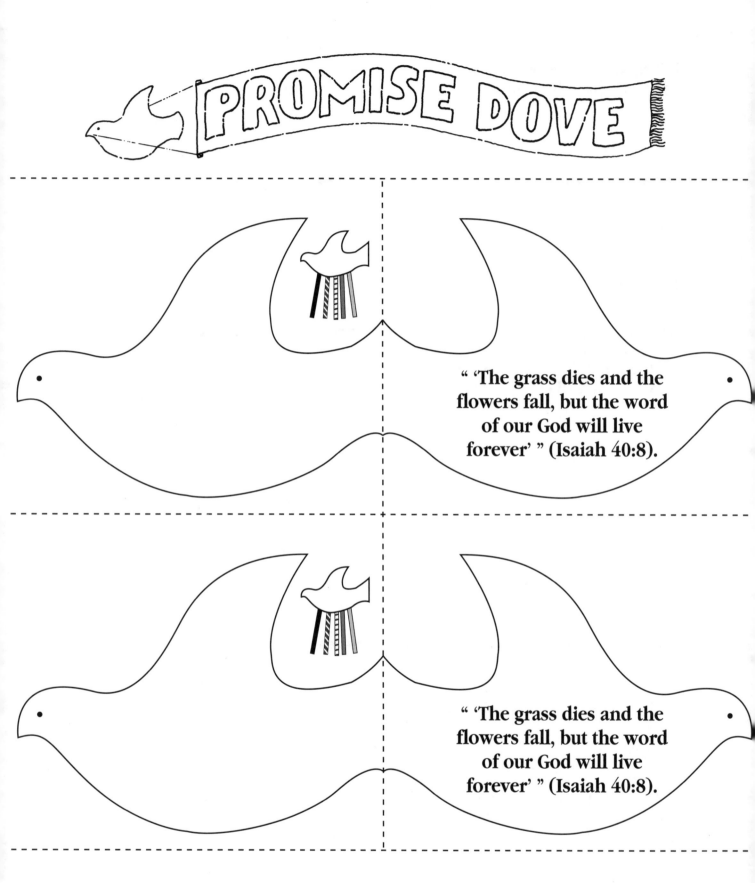

All Kinds of Families

6

LESSON AIM

To help kids learn that ★ families are important to God.

OBJECTIVES

Kids or families will
- do family role-plays with their wrists tied together,
- learn what effect bragging and jealousy had on Joseph's family,
- explore biblical ways to solve family problems, and
- commit to showing God's love in their families.

BIBLE BASIS

Genesis 37:1-36

There's no such thing as a perfect family. From the very beginning of Scripture, God points out human weaknesses that led to family feuds and the tragic consequences that followed. The stories of the patriarchs are filled with scheming, jealousy, and even murder.

When we look at the story of Joseph and his brothers, we probably get a little angry with Jacob for his obvious favoritism. But think back to Jacob's family of origin. Jacob was favored by his mother, Rebekah, while Isaac preferred Esau, Jacob's twin. Rebekah and Jacob schemed together to steal Esau's birthright. Pain and dysfunction went from generation to generation in ancient times, just as they do today.

God has a better plan—a plan of forgiveness and healing.

YOU'LL NEED

- ❏ 12-inch lengths of string or ribbon
- ❏ markers
- ❏ large paper grocery bags
- ❏ T-shirts
- ❏ sweat pants or shorts
- ❏ chocolate kisses
- ❏ towelettes or damp washcloths in sandwich bags
- ❏ scissors
- ❏ Bibles
- ❏ Bible costumes (optional)
- ❏ slips of paper
- ❏ a pencil
- ❏ photocopies of the "Funtastic Families" handout (p. 59)
- ❏ star stickers

NOTE

This lesson works well with an intergenerational class. You may wish to invite whole families to join you for this session.

Lesson 7 will deal with Joseph's perseverance and reconciliation with his brothers.

Ephesians 4:29–5:1

Unfortunately, most of us have a perverse tendency to save our worst behavior for those we love the most. These verses encourage a thoughtful, loving, forgiving mind-set. Help kids understand that home is the best place to learn to practice Christlike behavior.

UNDERSTANDING YOUR KIDS

Families come in all sizes and shapes. You'll need to be careful to see that kids from every kind of family situation feel accepted and "normal" in your class.

You're probably aware that kids whose parents are divorced often feel responsible for the problems in their families. It will be especially important to tactfully protect these kids from feeling singled out in any way during this lesson.

Kids can't be responsible for what other people in their families do. But children can make a positive difference in their families by making a commitment to love, forgive, and interact positively with the people in their homes.

The Lesson

ATTENTION GRABBER

Stuck Together

As people arrive, assign them to families. Make families as small as two or three, and as large as six or seven. If you've invited whole families to an intergenerational class, scramble them so no two members of a real family end up together.

Have the families you created sit together in a circle. Distribute 12-inch lengths of string or ribbon and have family members tie their wrists together with the people on their left and right.

When all the families are tied together in their own circles, give each family a marker and a large paper grocery bag containing a T-shirt, sweat pants or shorts, several chocolate kisses, and a towelette or damp washcloth in a sandwich bag.

Say: **Decide what you want your family's last name to**

TEACHER TIP

Warn kids not to tie their wrists together too tightly. If adults are with you for this class, it's best to use chairs for this activity. If your group is all kids, it's fine to have family groups sit on the floor.

be, then write it in big letters on your paper bag.

Acknowledge each of the family names by saying, "Oh, here are the Joneses" or "I see we have the Oglethorpe family here today. Welcome!"

Then say: **We're about to embark on a family adventure. I'll tell you what to do. You'll find all the things you need in your handy-dandy family bag. But don't look in the bag until I tell you what you need.**

Give families this series of commands:

● **Choose one person to be the baby. Dress the baby. Take the T-shirt out of the bag and slip it over the baby's head. Then find the sweat pants or shorts and help the baby put them on.**

● **Eat breakfast. Take the chocolate kisses out of the bag. Each person will unwrap one chocolate kiss and feed it to the person on his or her left.**

● **Drive to work and school. Stand up together and walk clockwise around the room until you come back to your original spot.**

● **Drive home. Stand up together and walk counterclockwise around the room until you come back to your original spot.**

● **Eat dinner. Unwrap a chocolate kiss and feed it to the person on your right.**

● **Clean up after dinner. Take the washcloth or towelette out of the sandwich bag and gently wipe the hands of the person on your left.**

After the families have completed all these activities, give an older child in each family a pair of scissors to cut the family members apart. Have families put their props back in their bags. Then gather everyone in a circle. Ask:

● **What was difficult about this activity?** (It was hard to do everything when we were all tied together.)

● **How were you able to accomplish everything I asked you to do?** (By working together; by cooperating.)

● **What happened if you couldn't agree on how to do something?** (It took us longer; we had to agree.)

● **How was this experience like what happens in your real families at home?** (We all have to work together; we have to help each other; we have to think about what other people need.)

Say: **As I watched you work in your family groups, it looked like you were having lots of fun. But sometimes you looked frustrated, and you had to work hard. It's the same with our families in real life. We have good times and hard times, and we all need to keep working together. Today we're going to learn some of what the**

Bible says about families because ★ families are important to God.

BIBLE STUDY

The Case of the Missing Brother (Genesis 37)

Set up a readers theater by placing four chairs at the corners of a large square. Choose one person to be Joseph; one to be Joseph's father, Jacob; one person to be Reuben; and one to be Judah. Ask each character to be seated in one of the chairs. Have everyone else sit in the middle of the square and take the role of the other brothers.

Say: **Let's open our Bibles to Genesis 37 to find out what happened to a very important family in the Bible. I'll be the narrator. I'll nod to the people playing Joseph, Jacob, Reuben, and Judah when it's their turn to read. The rest of you will be Joseph's other brothers. Every time you hear me read the word "brothers," say, "Mumble, mumble, mumble," as if you're angry.**

Read all of Genesis 37, cuing characters to read their parts at the appropriate times. Encourage the characters to read dramatically and add action to their parts.

After the reading, call for a big round of applause. Then ask:

● **Who do you feel sorry for in this story?** (Joseph, because he was sold as a slave; Jacob, because he lost his favorite son; the brothers, because their father played favorites.)

● **Whose fault was it that Joseph was sold as a slave?** (Joseph's, because he bragged; the brothers', because they were jealous; Jacob's, because he didn't treat all his children the same.)

Say: **When there's trouble in a family, we usually try to pin the blame on someone else. But saying it's someone else's fault doesn't solve anything. Usually everyone plays some part in the problem, just like in Joseph's family.** Ask:

● **Those of you who read special parts, what could your character have done to prevent what happened to Joseph at the end of this story?** (Jacob could have shown all his sons that he loved them; Joseph could have kept from bragging and showing off his special coat; Judah could have talked with the brothers about settling the problem a better way.)

Say: **When there's a family problem, everyone can**

work together to solve it. And that pleases God because ★ **God thinks families are important.**

LIFE APPLICATION

Pick a Fight

Write the following phrases on separate slips of paper:
- Whose turn it is to do the dishes.
- Doing homework before watching TV.
- Whether to watch a baseball game or a Disney movie.
- Whether to eat at McDonald's or Pizza Hut.
- Who gets to ride in the front seat.
- Who hogs the telephone.
- Borrowing someone's clothes without asking.
- Who's always the last one ready to go to school or church.

Have everyone re-form their family groups from the Attention Grabber. Give each family one slip of paper.

Say: **You have two minutes to prepare a family feud about what's written on your slip of paper. There are two rules. First, please don't use any bad language. Second, everyone in your family must be involved in your skit.**

After two minutes, call on families to give their skits. Give each group a hearty round of applause.

After all the groups have performed, say: **In your groups, read aloud Ephesians 4:29–5:1. Then, following the advice of those verses, plan a new ending to your skit.**

Allow about a minute for planning, then have groups perform once again.

Say: ★ **Families are important to God. That's why it's important to work together to solve problems, to show that you love each other, and to be ready to forgive.**

TEACHER TIP

If you have adults in your class, encourage them to take the roles of children in the skits. The role reversal can be quite entertaining!

TEACHER TIP

If you're running short of time, you may want to have family groups simply tell how their problems could be resolved rather than performing again.

COMMITMENT

Funtastic Families

Distribute photocopies of the "Funtastic Families" handout (p. 59). Have everyone draw or write about their real families in the center of the handout, then share with their family groups what they wrote or drew.

Say: **Now read through the funtastic-family ideas**

together and tell your family group members which idea you plan to do this week with your family at home.

CLOSING

Family Affirmations

As everyone is sharing, pass out star stickers.

Say: **Now take a moment to put a star sticker on each member of your family group. As you put the sticker on, say, "You're a funtastic family member because . . . ," then finish the sentence with something nice you've noticed about that person.**

As family groups finish their affirmations, gather everyone in a large circle for a group hug.

Pray: **Lord, thank you for all the different kinds of families we represent. I pray that you'll bless each family and help us all to show your love at home. In Jesus' name, amen.**

Draw or write about your family in the center of the page. Then follow this path to become a funtastic family. Put a star beside each idea you try.

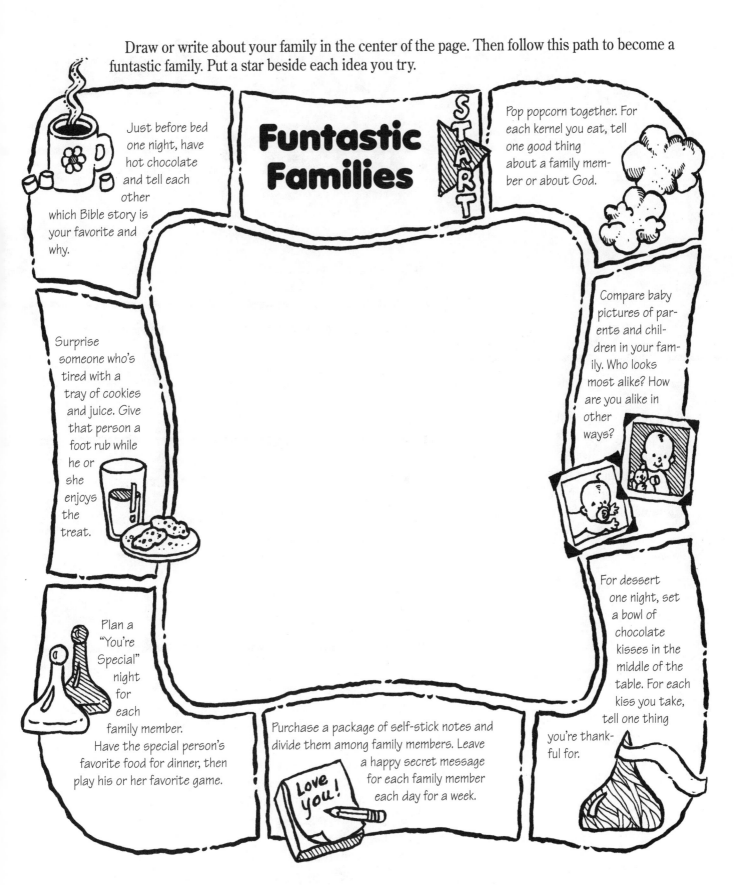

Funtastic Families

START

Pop popcorn together. For each kernel you eat, tell one good thing about a family member or about God.

Just before bed one night, have hot chocolate and tell each other which Bible story is your favorite and why.

Compare baby pictures of parents and children in your family. Who looks most alike? How are you alike in other ways?

Surprise someone who's tired with a tray of cookies and juice. Give that person a foot rub while he or she enjoys the treat.

For dessert one night, set a bowl of chocolate kisses in the middle of the table. For each kiss you take, tell one thing you're thankful for.

Plan a "You're Special" night for each family member. Have the special person's favorite food for dinner, then play his or her favorite game.

Purchase a package of self-stick notes and divide them among family members. Leave a happy secret message for each family member each day for a week.

Love you!

When Things Get Tough

YOU'LL NEED

- ❏ five containers of different sizes
- ❏ a plastic tablecloth
- ❏ masking tape
- ❏ marshmallows
- ❏ photocopies of the "Hard Times" handout (p. 67)
- ❏ pencils or markers

LESSON AIM

To help kids believe that ★ God will help us through hard times.

OBJECTIVES

Kids will
- ● experience receiving a prize that isn't what they had hoped for,
- ● act out Joseph's story of troubles and triumph,
- ● describe responses to tough situations, and
- ● commit to trusting God when they face tough times.

BIBLE BASIS

Genesis 39–45

It's impossible to read the story of Joseph without marveling at how he handled the incredible ups and downs of his life. Favorite son to slave. Favored servant to prisoner. Prisoner to second in command of all Egypt. Whew! Most amazing of all is Joseph's steady, level-headed dedication to serving God by doing his best in every circumstance.

In our culture we've come to believe that life owes us a steady job with good retirement income, a comfortable home, more than we need to eat, and regular opportunities for rest and recreation. If illness, loss of a job, or other financial setbacks come our way, we tend to think that God owes us an explanation.

Joseph might smile at us and shake his head. He didn't find

his security in his family or his job. Joseph was content to place his life in the hands of the living God who was as much present in a dark prison as in Pharaoh's palace.

In his adult years, Joseph stands out as one of the Bible's few sterling characters. There's no moral slip, no greed, no glaring faults—just a man who trusted God completely.

Psalm 37:3a, 5

"Trust the Lord and do good" is the Christian's response to every situation in life, good or bad, deserved or undeserved. We can trust God to bring us through no matter how defeating the circumstances may seem.

UNDERSTANDING YOUR KIDS

Few kids in Western societies realize how much their lifestyles contrast with those of people in less-privileged countries. But affluence doesn't necessarily result in contentment. No matter what their ages are, kids focus on the next gadget they plan to acquire rather than on the bounty they already enjoy.

Kids can learn a lot from the story of Joseph. He shifted from the ranks of the haves to those of the have-nots on a regular basis. Yet we don't hear a whisper of complaint. He always did his best, even when he was treated unfairly. Because he was so focused on God, Joseph could take the best and worst life had to offer.

Use this lesson to challenge kids to look for God's hand in every situation and to rely on God's strength when the going gets tough.

The Lesson

ATTENTION GRABBER

No Fair!

Set up a marshmallow-toss using five containers set in a line, the smallest container in front and the largest in back. Any containers will do. You might start with a #2 tin can and end with a bucket, adding three other containers of increasingly large sizes in between. Spread a plastic tablecloth under the containers so kids will be able to eat the marshmallows that bounce on the floor.

Place one masking tape line on the floor two feet from the first container and a second line three feet from the first container. Younger kids will toss from the closer line, and older kids from the farther.

As kids arrive, give them each five marshmallows.

Say: **I have great prizes for kids who can toss their marshmallows into all five containers.**

Have each student try to toss a marshmallow in each container. After kids have each had their turn, let them retrieve their marshmallows from the containers or from the floor, but don't allow them to eat their marshmallows yet.

After everyone has played, congratulate the kids who got all or most of their marshmallows in the containers.

Then say: **I promised great prizes for getting all your marshmallows in the containers. Here's your prize: You get to eat your marshmallows. By the way, everyone else can eat their marshmallows, too.**

When kids protest, ask:

● **What's wrong?** (This isn't fair; you promised us a great prize, but kids who didn't win got the same thing we did.)

Say: **Hmm. This isn't what you expected, is it? But, you see, when I promised you a prize, I never said that the other kids wouldn't get a prize, too.**

Ask:

● **Do you still think it's unfair? Why or why not?** (Yes, because I think we should get a better prize; no, because this way everyone gets a treat.)

Say: **Sometimes life surprises us in ways we think are unfair. For instance, you might study hard for a test but get a poor grade. You might get blamed for something you didn't do. Or someone you trust might fail to keep a promise. It seems unfair, but there's not a whole lot you can do about it. The good news is that ★ God helps us through tough times.**

BIBLE STUDY

Troubles and Triumph (Genesis 37; 39; 41–45)

Say: **Today's Bible story is about a young man who had one tough time after another, and none of it was really his fault. I'll tell the story as a ballad. Watch me carefully and do exactly what I do.**

Read "The Favorite Son" (pp. 64-65) and do the motions in parentheses.

Give a round of applause for kids' participation in the story. Then ask:

● **What happened to Joseph that was especially hard or unfair?** (He was sold as a slave; he was put in prison for something he didn't do.)

● **Suppose you were put in prison even though you'd never committed a crime. How would you feel? What would you do?** (I'd be angry; I'd try to break out.)

● **What special things did Joseph do?** (He still did his best, even though bad things happened to him; he forgave his brothers even though they'd been really mean to him; he saved up enough food for everyone.)

● **Why do you think Joseph could do all these good things even when bad things kept happening to him?** (He trusted God; he knew God would work things out.)

Say: ★ **God will help us through hard times. Joseph knew that. Because Joseph trusted God, he kept doing his best in every situation. And that's not always easy to do. Let's explore ways we can follow Joseph's example today.**

LIFE APPLICATION

Hard Times

Distribute photocopies of the "Hard Times" handout (p. 67). Help kids form three groups. Assign each group one of the articles on the handout. Have a volunteer read aloud the verse at the top of the handout.

Then say: **This verse could be Joseph's motto! Joseph was always willing to trust God and do good.**

In just a moment, I'll have you read through your article together and decide how the people in your story could trust God and do good, just as Joseph did.

Explain that each group will need a reader to read the article aloud, a reporter to share the group's discussion with the rest of the class, and several encouragers to make sure everyone gets involved in the discussion.

Call time after about three minutes. Have the reporters tell how their groups decided the people in their stories could trust God and do good.

After each report, open the discussion to the rest of the class and encourage the whole class to brainstorm other ways to trust God and do good in that situation.

TEACHER TIP

Rehearse the ballad several times before class so you can do the motions along with the story. Or, choose an older student to tell the story with you. The student can lead the motions as you read the ballad.

If you taught lesson 6 last week, say: **Last week we learned how Joseph's brothers sold him as a slave. Today we're going to review that story, then see what happened to Joseph next.**

TEACHER TIP

Explain that readers and reporters don't necessarily have to be older kids. Encourage groups to give responsibility to younger kids as well.

The Favorite Son
(from Genesis 37; 39; 41–45)

Fathers, brothers, sisters, mothers.
Me, my cat, my dog, and others.
Grandmas, uncles, aunts, and cousins.
Family members by the dozens.
How many people live with you?
Eleven or 12, or one or two?

Joseph lived with many others.
Joseph had 11 brothers!
(Count on fingers as you name the
brothers.)
Brothers Levi, Asher, Dan,
Judah, Gad, and Simeon.
Reuben, Issachar, Benjamin.
Naphtali and Zebulun.
But Joseph was the favorite son—
his father Jacob's #1.
(Hold up one finger.)

Jacob gave his son a coat.
A brand new coat—then he could gloat.
(Pretend to hold up a coat.)
Joseph had more than the others—
there were no coats for his brothers.
Joseph's coat was the only one,
for Joseph was the favorite son.
(Hug yourself.)

That special coat was quite a sight!
(Make glasses with your fingers.)
Colorful and very bright.
Purple, yellow, pink, and green—
the prettiest coat you've ever seen.
Joseph's coat fit perfectly!
It's beautiful, don't you agree?

The other brothers made a fuss.
(Put hands on hips.)

"Why does he get more than us?"
They began to grumble and pout.
(Make a sour face.)
"Why did father leave us out?"
Tell me now what you would do
if there'd been no gift for you.
One night Joseph had a dream—
his brothers all bowed down to him!
(Bow down.)
The older boys had had enough,
so they decided to get rough.
(Hold up fists.)
"This favorite son has got to go!
Then maybe Dad will love us, too."

The boys threw Joseph in a well.
(Look down.)
Then decided they would tell
old Jacob that his son had died.
That would fix young Joseph's pride!
Then a caravan came by.
The boys said, "Hey—why don't we try
to sell our brother for some money?
Joseph a slave! Isn't that funny?"
(Hold your stomach and laugh.)

His brothers got him in a mess,
but Joseph chose to try his best.
And all along he thought, "You'll see
(point upward)—
the Lord, my God, will set me free."

Even when Joseph was a slave,
he was kind and smart and brave.
Then someone nasty told a tale,
and Joseph ended up in jail!
(Wrap hands around imaginary bars.)
But still he didn't

(continued)

moan or pout—
he trusted God to work things out.

One day Joseph got a call
to see King Pharaoh in his hall.
(Make a crown with your hands.)
The king was troubled by his dreams.
(Frown.)
He said, "Please tell me what this means."
Joseph helped him understand
that God in heaven had a plan.

"For seven years you'll have good crops
(thumbs up),
but after that, the growing stops.
(Thumbs down.)
Get someone to make a plan
to save up all the food you can."
The king said, "Joseph, you're my man!
(Point.)
I'll make you second in command."

Now that Joseph was in charge,
he built new barns that were quite large.
(Spread arms.)
He gathered food from everywhere
so there would be enough to share.
Then when the ground grew hard and dry,
people came to him to buy.
(Hold out a hand.)

Joseph's brothers came one day.
They traveled there from far away
to get some food for their empty bowls
(cup empty hands)
and stop their stomachs' hungry growls.
(Rub stomach.)

As they bowed before their brother
(bow down),

they mistook him for another.
They didn't see him as the one
who'd been their father's favorite son.
So Joseph tested them to find
(rub your chin)
if their hearts were mean or kind.

Joseph's brothers passed the test.
He knew they wanted what was best.
Joseph hugged them, one by one
(give hugs),
and then before the day was done,
he filled their baskets with good food.
(Circle arms like a basket.)
More and more—they overflowed!

When Joseph's brothers went to pack
(wave goodbye),
they promised to bring their father back.
The family moved to Egypt, where
they lived their lives in Joseph's care.
Then their days were filled with laughter,
and they lived happily ever after.
(Fold arms and nod.)

My Times

Say: **The God who took care of Joseph during all his ups and downs is the same God who takes care of us today. ★ God will help us through hard times, just as he helped Joseph.**

Distribute pencils or markers. Help kids find partners. Make it a point to match older kids with younger partners, and shy kids with outgoing partners.

Say: **There's a blank space on your Hard Times newspaper where you can write or draw your own story. You can tell about a tough situation you faced in the past, one that you're facing right now, or a tough situation you may face in the future. I'll give you about three minutes to write or draw. Then I'll call time and ask you to share your story with your partner.**

After three minutes, call time and have kids share their stories with their partners.

Then say: **Now tell your partner how you could trust God and do good in this situation.**

After partners have shared, bring everyone together. Invite volunteers to tell about their partners' situations and how they could trust God in the midst of them.

CLOSING

Trust Pileup

Have kids form a circle, place their handouts on the floor behind them, and link arms.

Say: **Because Joseph trusted God and did his best, thousands and thousands of lives were saved during the great famine. Joseph was just one person. If all of us promise to trust God and do good, think of the good things that could happen. ★ God will help us through hard times. Let's celebrate that by making a pile of hands. When you add your hand to the pile, say, "Trust God and do good!"**

When all the hands are on the pile, pray: **Dear Lord, thank you for the way you helped Joseph through hard times. Help us to trust you and do good, just as Joseph did. Amen.**

TEACHER TIP

Circulate among the kids as they work on their stories. Brainstorm with kids who have trouble getting started.

HARD TIMES

"Trust the Lord and do good. Depend on the Lord; trust him, and he will take care of you" (Psalm 37:3a, 5).

GIRL ACCUSED OF CHEATING

Miss Wompet made Greta Goodgrade stay after school today and miss soccer practice. "Miss Wompet thought I was cheating," Greta reported, "but I wasn't. The person behind me asked how much more time we had to finish our test. I said we had five minutes, but I didn't tell any answers. Now I won't be able to play in this weekend's soccer game because I have to miss today's practice."

FLU CANCELS CAMP PLANS

Several kids from Neighborhood Church had to cancel plans to attend camp when they came down with the flu earlier this week. The group had worked hard to earn money for camp. They had held a carwash, a bake sale, and an auction. "With many of the kids already sick and others exposed to the flu, we decided to cancel camp plans entirely," Pastor Will U. Begood reported.

FLOOD WASHES OUT HOMES

Several area homes were damaged in flash floods over the weekend. "The river just couldn't handle all the rain," said Hi N. Dry, a local builder. "It'll be weeks before things are back to normal." The Red Cross has set up temporary shelters for the flood victims in local churches. "I just want to go home," said one 8-year-old at the Red Cross shelter. "I was supposed to have my birthday party tomorrow."

ADD YOUR STORY HERE

Faith to Give Away

8

YOU'LL NEED

- ❏ bubbles and a bubble wand
- ❏ a noisemaker
- ❏ Bibles
- ❏ a photocopy of the "Bible-Story Name Tags" handout (p. 74)
- ❏ scissors
- ❏ safety pins
- ❏ a gift-wrapped box of bubble gum
- ❏ photocopies of the "Treasure Slips" handout (p. 75)
- ❏ aluminum foil
- ❏ ribbon

LESSON AIM

To help kids understand that ★ it's important to tell others about God's love.

OBJECTIVES

Kids will
- ● learn how Naaman's servant girl told about God's prophet,
- ● explore the treasures God offers those who believe in Jesus, and
- ● commit to caring for people by looking for opportunities to share their faith.

BIBLE BASIS

2 Kings 5:1-17

This is a touching story of faith and devotion from an unexpected source. Foreign soldiers kidnap a Hebrew girl in a raid, then carry her off to work in the home of the army's commander. You'd think the child would be sullen and rebellious—ready to escape or sabotage her captors at the first opportunity. But, amazingly, this nameless girl cares for her master and urges him to go to Elisha for a cure for leprosy. Talk about loving your enemies!

We often think of sharing our faith as orally explaining God's plan of redemption. But let's not put such a crucial element of our faith life in such a small box. The girl in the story witnessed by caring about her master's illness and expressing her faith that God's prophet could heal him. This is the key: We share our faith in any number of ways because we truly care about people and want to point them to the living God.

Romans 10:14-15
It doesn't require a seminary degree to share with others the good news that Jesus offers us forgiveness and the opportunity to become children of God. The news we have to share is good news! Let's not keep it to ourselves!

UNDERSTANDING YOUR KIDS

Did you ever try to shut down a group of kids who were really excited about something? It's close to impossible! That's what makes kids so great. They're sincere and transparent and full of energy. So when they get excited about their walk with God, watch out! Great things will happen.

How do you get them excited? Let them see how God works in people's lives. Keep them in touch with the prayer life of your church. Involve them in faith-building activities in which they can make a difference, such as a workday at the home of an elderly friend or a visit to an interfaith community-service center. Let kids come face to face with people whose lives are being changed by God's power.

Use this lesson to help kids see that they can make a difference in people's lives by sharing their faith both orally and in creative, practical ways.

The Lesson

ATTENTION GRABBER

Sob Tag
Choose one person to be "It" and another person to be the "healer." Give the healer a bottle of bubbles and a bubble wand.

Say: **We're going to start today with a new game called Sob Tag. If It tags you, you have to kneel down and start crying and sobbing. The only way you can stop sobbing is if the healer blows bubbles over your** head. One more thing—no one can run in this game. Everyone moves around the room by taking giant steps, the biggest steps you can possibly take. Let's all practice sobbing before we get started.

Demonstrate crying and sobbing for the kids. Then say: **Great! You guys sound really sad. Let's play. Remember—no running. Ready to begin? Go!**

Every minute or so shake a noisemaker and allow different students to take the roles of It and the healer. Before kids begin to tire, stop the game with the noisemaker, then have kids take three deep breaths and sit down. Set the bubbles out of sight. Ask:

● **What was fun about this game?** (It was different playing Tag with giant steps; it sounded funny with everybody sobbing; it was fun to get bubbles blown on me.)

● **What was it like to sob and sob?** (I got tired of it; it was hard not to laugh.)

● **When do people cry like that in real life?** (When they've had an accident; when something terrible happens.)

● **What was it like to be the healer?** (I wanted to hurry and get to everyone; it was hard to keep ahead of It.)

● **Can you think of anyone in real life who's like the healer in our game? Explain.** (Jesus; doctors heal people; people in ambulances and firetrucks have to hurry to help people in emergencies.)

Say: **In our Bible story we'll find out about a prophet who had special healing power from God. He didn't need bubbles! But the real hero in the story is a bit of a surprise. Listen carefully and, at the end of the story, tell me who you think the hero is. Here's a hint: ★ It's important to tell others about God's love.**

BIBLE STUDY

A Little Girl Who Cared (2 Kings 5:1-17)

Read this Bible story straight from an easy-to-understand version of the Bible. Photocopy the "Bible-Story Name Tags" handout (p. 74) and cut apart the name tags for the characters in the story. Assign the roles by pinning a name tag on the student who will read that character's part. Then be prepared to cue the readers when their parts come up in the text.

Have the characters sit in a semicircle in front of the class with the rest of the students facing them.

Say to the kids who don't have a part: **You have two things to do. This story is about a man named Naaman**

TEACHER TIP

If some characters have trouble with their parts, consider reading through the story a second time.

who was a great general, so each time you hear his name, say, "Yes, sir!"

Practice the name and response with the kids.

Then say: **Good job. Now you have one more thing to do. This story has two kings in it. Each time you hear the word "king," say, "May you live forever!" That's what people said in Old Testament times to show respect. Let's try that. King!** (May you live forever.) **Great! Now let's get on with the story. Don't forget to listen for who the real hero is. Narrator, you're on!**

Finish the story with a big round of applause. Then ask:

● **OK—who would you say is the hero of this story?** Accept all answers and have kids tell why they chose a particular character.

Say: **My choice for the hero of this story is the little servant girl.**

● **Why do you think I chose her?** (Because she told her master about Elisha; because she cared for people even though she was a slave.)

Say: **I don't know about you, but if I got kidnapped from my home and was forced to work in another family, I think I might be a little unfriendly to the people I had to work for.** Ask:

● **Why do you think this little servant girl wanted to help her master?** (She was a kind, loving person; maybe her master's family was nice to her; she believed in God and wanted others to believe in God, too.)

Say: **Isn't it interesting that we don't even know the little girl's name? But what we do know about her is pretty important. She cared enough about her master to tell him what God's prophet could do. And ★ it's important to tell others about God's love.**

LIFE APPLICATION

Bub-Bub-Bub-Bubblin'!

Put enough bubble gum in a box for each child to have two or three pieces. Gift-wrap the box and place it where children will see it and wonder about it.

Pick up the box and say: **Hmm. I think I've kept you in suspense long enough. It's about time to give this away. I wonder who'll catch it.** Turn your back to the children and toss the box over your shoulder.

If more than one child grabs for the box, say: **Don't worry—I think there'll be plenty for everyone.**

71

Invite the child who caught the box to open it. Let everyone peek inside. Then have the child who opened the box help you toss pieces of bubble gum to everyone. Put a piece of bubble gum in your mouth and say: **I wonder if anyone can blow a bubble faster than I can!**

Have kids gather in a circle as they all blow bubbles. Then say: **Let's all blow one more bubble together. Then when I pop my bubble, you pop yours, too.**

After all the bubbles have popped, ask:

● **How was what** (name of the child who caught the box) **did like what the little girl in the Bible story did?** (He shared the good thing with others; she didn't keep the good thing to herself.)

● **What would've happened if the little girl in the story hadn't told her master about what God could do?** (He would've died; he would've been in pain for the rest of his life.)

● **What would've happened if** (name of child) **had kept all the bubble gum?** (I would've been sad; I would've asked for some.)

● **How is that like what happens if we don't tell others about God's love?** (They are left out; they don't know about God's forgiveness and the other good things they're missing.)

Have a volunteer look up and read Romans 10:14-15. Ask:

● **What does this verse mean to you?** (People need a chance to hear about God before they can believe; people can't believe in God if they've never heard of him.)

Say: **Having Jesus in our lives makes us so happy that we want to share it with everyone. We just bubble over! Quickly find a partner and blow bubbles together. Then pop your bubbles and tell each other the name of one person you want to share God's love with this week. Ready? Set? Blow!**

COMMITMENT

Hidden Treasure

Before class, photocopy the "Treasure Slips" handout (p. 75), cut the slips apart, and wrap them in aluminum foil in the shape of chocolate kisses. Tie a small bow around the neck of each one, then hide the "treasures" around the room.

Shake the noisemaker to bring everyone together. Ask:

● **What good thing happened to Naaman after he**

heard about the true God? (He was healed.)

Say: **Do you know that something even better than that happens to everyone who hears about Jesus and believes in him? A whole bunch of really good things happen. I've hidden some of those things around the room. There are seven hidden treasures for you to find. Nobody can claim more than one. When you find a treasure, bring it to me. When you've found all seven treasures, we'll open them together.**

Let the children open and read the treasures. If a nonreader finds a treasure, let him or her choose an older child to read it to the class.

After all seven treasure slips have been read aloud, say: ★ **It's important to tell others about God's love—starting with your very own family. So let's make treasures you can share with your family this week—one treasure slip per day.**

Distribute scissors, pieces of aluminum foil, and photocopies of the "Treasure Slips" handout (p. 75). Have kids cut apart the treasure slips. As they're cutting, place another piece of bubble gum beside each person.

Say: **Put the bubble gum in the center of your foil. Then twist the foil around the treasure slips in the shape of a big chocolate kiss. You can put your treasure on your table at home. Each night, have someone in your family pull out a treasure slip. Then look up the Bible verse and read it together. On the last night, pull out the bubble gum and tell how you bubbled over telling others about God's love during the week.**

TEACHER TIP

If you have time, have volunteers look up and read the verses referred to on the treasure slips.

CLOSING

Treasure Circle

Have kids stand in a circle holding their treasures. Pray: **Dear Lord, thank you for all these treasures you give us when we believe in you. We know ★ it's important to tell others about God's love. Help us bubble over and share your wonderful treasures with others this week. In Jesus' name, amen.**

BIBLE-STORY NAME TAGS

Narrator

Servant Girl

King of Aram

King of Israel

Elisha

Messenger

Naaman

Naaman's Servant

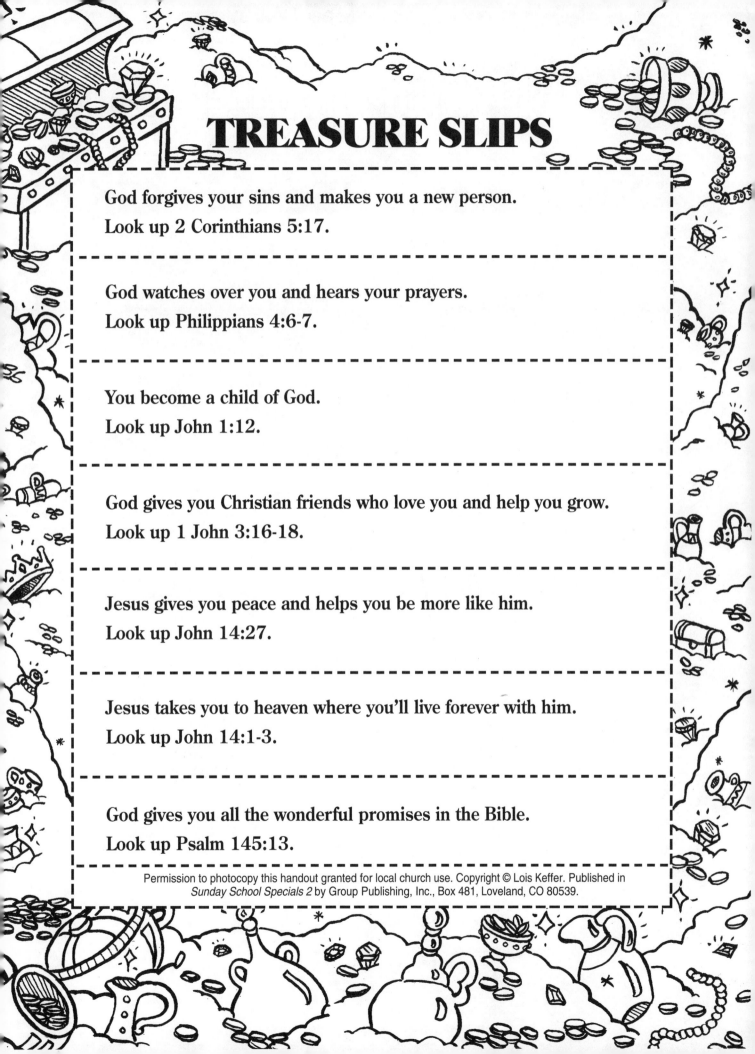

TREASURE SLIPS

God forgives your sins and makes you a new person.
Look up 2 Corinthians 5:17.

God watches over you and hears your prayers.
Look up Philippians 4:6-7.

You become a child of God.
Look up John 1:12.

God gives you Christian friends who love you and help you grow.
Look up 1 John 3:16-18.

Jesus gives you peace and helps you be more like him.
Look up John 14:27.

Jesus takes you to heaven where you'll live forever with him.
Look up John 14:1-3.

God gives you all the wonderful promises in the Bible.
Look up Psalm 145:13.

Celebrating
Special Times

Thank You, Lord!

(a lesson for Thanksgiving or any time)

LESSON AIM

To help kids learn that ★ it's good to give thanks.

OBJECTIVES

Kids or families will
- experience not being thanked for their efforts, then being thanked;
- examine and re-create the Feast of Tabernacles;
- create personal expressions of thanks to God; and
- commit to a thankful lifestyle.

BIBLE BASIS

Deuteronomy 16:13-17; Nehemiah 8:13-18

The Feast of Tabernacles is a fascinating Jewish festival and an interesting parallel to our Thanksgiving. Unlike our Thanksgiving celebration, the Feast of Tabernacles lasted seven days, from the 15th to the 21st day of Tishri, our October. During this feast the Israelites traveled to Jerusalem where they celebrated the harvest of fruits and olives. They built and camped out in outdoor shelters called "booths" to commemorate the 40 years their ancestors had lived in temporary shelters as they wandered in the wilderness. Shelters were located on rooftops, in courtyards, in the court of the

YOU'LL NEED

- ❏ sheets, blankets, or small tents
- ❏ Bibles
- ❏ newsprint
- ❏ a marker
- ❏ a toy horn
- ❏ a cassette tape or CD of Jewish choruses
- ❏ a cassette or CD player
- ❏ grapes, olives, dates, and soda crackers
- ❏ juice
- ❏ paper cups and plates
- ❏ photocopies of the "Thankful Turkey" handout (p. 85)
- ❏ pencils
- ❏ scissors
- ❏ old newspapers or scrap paper

NOTE

This lesson works well with an intergenerational class. You may wish to invite whole families to join you for this session.

temple, and along the edges of city streets. In the evenings the people lit torches and danced and sang in the streets. On the eighth day, they took the shelters down and gathered at the temple to worship.

It's wonderful to celebrate God's goodness with feasting. The key to making our Thanksgiving a holy celebration is to focus more on God's goodness than on the feast! It's good to give thanks any time of year. It's good to give thanks every day, several times a day. We live in a privileged time in privileged nations. The effects of wind or insect damage, droughts, and floods are seldom felt as we load our plates at dinner. Our distance from nature tends to dull our sense of dependence on God. Let's celebrate God's goodness and fully acknowledge that God is the giver of all good things!

Psalm 67

The psalms are rich with praise and are meaningful for people of all generations and all nations. This psalm celebrates God's goodness with joy and thanksgiving for a good harvest and God's blessing on his world.

UNDERSTANDING YOUR KIDS

Are there kids in your class who act as if coming to church is a chore? You can help them learn otherwise. Our culture constantly bombards kids with new and exciting entertainment, and it's hard for church to compete. But we have something much better to offer than entertainment: We can introduce kids and their families to the living God.

Worship and thanksgiving cut through high-tech hype and artificial values. Worship helps kids discover that "I am one little human being on one small planet in a galaxy in a universe that no one can comprehend, and the God who made all this demonstrates his love by taking care of me."

Now that's reason to give thanks!

The Lesson ATTENTION GRABBER

Thanks/No Thanks

During this lesson, participants will put together "booths"

to re-create the biblical Feast of Tabernacles. The booths can be made by simply draping sheets or blankets over tables and chairs, by putting up lightweight tents, or even by hanging small tents from the ceiling. Make the process as simple or as sophisticated as you like.

You'll need one booth for every four to six people. Decide where you'll have the booths set up—in the corners of the room, for instance. Leave the room in its usual configuration for the Attention Grabber.

When participants arrive, have everyone who has shoes that tie stand against one wall. Have everyone with slip-on shoes stand against the opposite wall. It's OK if the groups are unequal in size.

Turn to the group with shoes that tie and say: **Ties, I'd like you to help me rearrange the tables and chairs. Please move them to the other end of the room.**

After they perform this task, shrug your shoulders and shake your head.

Then turn to the other group and say: **OK, no-ties, I've changed my mind. I really liked the tables and chairs the way they were. Would you put them back, please?** When the no-ties finish their task, thank them enthusiastically. Pat them on their backs and shake hands with several of them.

Turn back to the ties and say: **OK, now I've got it figured out. I need one table in each corner** (or however you want to arrange the room for creating the booths) **and the chairs here in a semicircle.**

When the ties complete this task, say: **That's a great job! Thanks for sticking with me! I really appreciate your helpful attitude.**

Have everyone sit down, then ask:

● **Ties, how did it feel when you did what I asked without being thanked for it?** (Kind of disappointing; a little confusing.)

● **How did you feel when I did say thank you?** (I was glad that I helped you; I felt appreciated.)

● **How do you react when you do something nice for someone but that person doesn't thank you?** (It's OK, because it was my choice to help; I might not feel so friendly toward that person again.)

● **Who can tell me about a time when you got a note or other special thank-you from someone? How did that make you feel?** (Special; important; appreciated.)

Say: ★ **It's good to give thanks. We like it when people thank us for what we do, and we sometimes feel**

TEACHER TIP

If adults will be involved with the class, women in dresses who might feel uncomfortable sitting on the floor in booths can participate by being "feast makers."

bad if people don't notice or don't care. God likes it when we thank him, too. Today we're going to learn about a special feast the Israelites celebrated to give thanks to God.

BIBLE STUDY

Welcome to the Feast! (Deuteronomy 16:13-17; Nehemiah 8:13-18; Psalm 67)

Say: **Let's find out about this feast straight from the Bible. Listen carefully to what the Bible says, because I'm going to ask you what it tells us to do for our feast.**

Have volunteers read aloud Deuteronomy 16:13-17 and Nehemiah 8:13-18. Then ask:

● **What do we need to do to celebrate the Feast of Tabernacles?** (Build booths; read from the Bible; celebrate joyfully; thank God for the harvest; bring gifts.)

List participants' answers on a sheet of newsprint.

Say: **Before you leave class today, we'll do all these things. Let's begin by asking God to bless our feast time.**

Ask a volunteer to pray or pray a simple prayer yourself, asking God to bless your time of giving thanks.

After the prayer, bring out your toy horn and blow it. Explain that Jewish priests used to blow a ram's horn to call people to worship, and that whenever you blow your horn, everyone should stop what they're doing and focus on you.

Then say: **Now we need to build our booths.**

Help participants form groups of four to six people. Ask each group to choose a feast maker, a reader, and two or more booth builders. Show the readers and the booth builders the materials you've provided for making booths— tents to assemble or sheets and blankets to drape over tables and chairs. As the groups work, play lively, Jewish-sounding choruses. ("Cornerstone," "Humble Thyself in the Sight of the Lord," and "King of Kings" from *The Group Songbook* cassettes and CDs are good examples.)

As the readers and booth builders work on the booths, set out grapes, olives, dates, soda crackers, juice, paper cups, and paper plates. Have the feast makers prepare a plate of food and cups of juice for the people in their groups.

When the booths are complete and the feast prepared, blow the toy horn to bring everyone together. Say: **It's time for the feast! The food we have here is like foods people enjoyed in Bible times. Help your feast maker carry the** feast into your booth. Readers, before anyone eats, please read Psalm 67 aloud. At the end of the psalm, say "amen" together. Then enjoy your feast. ★ It's good to give thanks!

LIFE APPLICATION

Thankful Turkeys

Allow up to five minutes for groups to read Scripture and enjoy the Bible-time foods. Then blow the horn to get everyone's attention.

Say: **Stay in your booths. In just a moment, I'm going to ask you to send one of your booth builders to come pick up pencils, scissors, and photocopies of the "Thankful Turkey" handout (p. 85). You'll find directions for writing your own psalm of thanks on the handout. The readers and writers in your group can help those who don't yet read and write complete their handouts. When you're finished, read each other the psalms you've written.**

Have each group send a booth builder to pick up supplies. As participants work, circulate among the booths to offer encouragement and suggestions.

As you see groups finishing, blow the horn and announce that there are two minutes left. Then blow the horn again to bring everyone together. Invite volunteers to read their psalms to the whole group.

After volunteers have shared, say:**★ It's good to give thanks! All of us have different things we're thankful for and different ways of showing our thanks. Let's give thanks together by singing a song.**

Lead the group in a favorite song or chorus of thanksgiving.

COMMITMENT

Paper Offerings

Refer to the list you created that describes the Feast of Tabernacles. Point out that you've done most of the things on the list. Ask:

● **What do we need to do to complete our celebration?** (Give gifts to God.)

Set out piles of old newspapers or scrap paper. Have participants crumple, cut, or tear the paper to create sculptures of things they're thankful for. You might demonstrate by making a crumpled paper sculpture in front of the class.

Allow two or three minutes for participants to work. Then say: **Let's line up and present our sculptures to God as gifts of thanks.**

Lead the procession by walking to the front of the room, placing your sculpture on the table, and saying: **God, I thank you for** (whatever your sculpture represents). Then walk to the back of the room and signal the next participant to go forward. Encourage an atmosphere of quiet worship.

CLOSING

Thankful Lives

After all the sculptures have been presented, gather everyone around them.

Say: ★ **It's good to give thanks! And we don't have to wait for a feast day to do it. Turn to a person beside you and brainstorm three or four ways you can give thanks every day.**

Allow a minute for partners to share, then invite volunteers to share their ideas with the class.

Close with a prayer similar to this one: **Lord, you truly are a great God. Thank you for all the ways you show that you love us. Thank you for the good food we have to eat and the wonderful country we live in. Help us to remember to thank you every day. In Jesus' name, amen.**

Tell participants you'd be very thankful for help in taking down the booths. Encourage everyone to take their sculptures with them as reminders of God's goodness.

THANKFUL TURKEY

Create your own psalm of thanks by finishing the sentences below. Then cut on the heavy lines and fold on the dotted lines. Write your name on the heart that forms when you fold the handout.

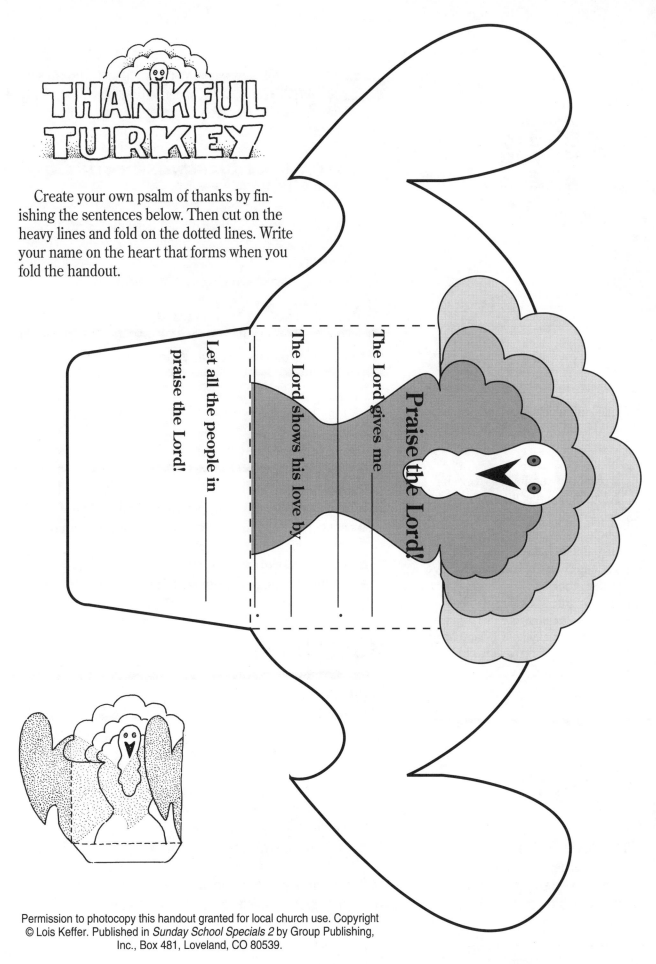

Let all the people in _____ praise the Lord!

The Lord shows his love by _____

The Lord gives me _____

Praise the Lord!

God With Us

(a lesson for Christmas or for Christmas in July)

YOU'LL NEED

- ❑ masking tape or garlands
- ❑ Christmas ornaments or candy canes
- ❑ blindfolds
- ❑ a photocopy of the "One Special Night" story (pp. 90-91)
- ❑ scissors
- ❑ photocopies of the "Symbols of Christmas" handout (pp. 94-97)
- ❑ various colors of construction paper or felt
- ❑ glue or glue sticks
- ❑ dowels (optional)
- ❑ cassettes or CDs of Christmas music
- ❑ cassette player or CD player

TEACHER TIP

This lesson works well with an intergenerational class. You may wish to invite whole families to join you for this session.

LESSON AIM

To help kids understand that ★ Jesus' birth means God is with us.

OBJECTIVES

Kids or families will
- ● experience having someone guide them,
- ● participate in an interactive story about the birth of Christ,
- ● learn about Christmas symbols and create a banner, and
- ● commit to being aware of God's presence in their lives.

BIBLE BASIS

Matthew 1:18-25

Immanuel. First spoken by Isaiah in his Messianic prophecy, "Immanuel" is one of Scripture's most profoundly beautiful words. It means, simply, "God with us." Since the beginning of the world, God has desired to be with us. Genesis 3:8-9 says, "Then they heard the Lord God walking in the garden during the cool part of the day, and the man and his wife hid from the Lord God among the trees in the garden. But the Lord God called to the man and said, 'Where are you?' " Sin had disrupted their fellowship. God gave the Law to define sin and point the way toward holiness. But only the incarnation of God's own Son could make it possible for God to truly be with us.

Jesus walked on earth to show us who God is. Jesus died to redeem us from our sins. Jesus rose again to conquer death and give us eternal life. Jesus sent the Holy Spirit to guide and empower us. Immanuel, God with us. What a gift!

Luke 2:11-12

The angel gave the shepherds a sign to recognize the Christ child: He would be wrapped in cloths and lying in a manger. We can be a sign to fellow Christians and to the world that the Christ of Christmas is with us today!

UNDERSTANDING YOUR KIDS

Kids in today's society learn to be on their own at an early age. They rehearse important "home alone" rules with their parents. By first grade many kids know how to be safe as they walk home from school, how to use the house key to let themselves in, how to fix themselves a snack, and how to call Mom or Dad to report that they're safe at home. Can you see how the concept that "God is with us" is an important one for these kids?

There's so much to be excited about at Christmas—even when it's Christmas in July! But the very best news you can give your kids is that God is truly with them, whether they're home alone, on a crowded school bus, confronting a neighborhood bully, or feeling secure with Mom and Dad close by. God's presence is the best of all presents!

The Lesson

ATTENTION GRABBER

Christmas Lane

Set up an obstacle course with Christmas decorations. Use garlands or masking tape to mark edges of a path about 3 feet wide and 15 feet long. Strew Christmas ornaments or candy canes along the path.

Pair up participants as they arrive, matching older kids or adults with younger kids. Have pairs decide which partner will be the walker and which will be the guide. Blindfold all the walkers.

Say: **Walkers, your job is to walk down Christmas Lane without stepping on any candy canes** (or ornaments). **Guides, your job is to talk your partner through the lane. You may not touch your partner—just walk alongside and tell him or her where to step.**

After the first walker is a few feet into the path, have the next walker begin. When each pair finishes the path, greet the partners with applause and remove the walker's blindfold. If you have plenty of time, you may want to let the walkers and guides switch roles. When everyone has finished, gather the group and ask:

● **What was it like to walk through Christmas Lane blindfolded?** (Scary; exciting.)

● **Walkers, how did you feel about your guides?** (I trusted her; I hoped he would tell me the right thing.)

● **What would've happened if you hadn't had a guide?** (I might've tripped or broken something; I wouldn't have been able to stay on the path.)

● **Guides, how did you feel about your walkers?** (I wanted to take good care of him; I tried really hard to tell her where to step.)

● **How is what the guides did like what God does for his followers?** (God tells us how to live; God's words keep us on the right path.)

● **When the prophet Isaiah foretold Jesus' birth, he said Jesus would be called "Immanuel." Can anyone tell me what "Immanuel" means?** (God with us.)

● **Why would Jesus be called that?** (Because he is God, and he came to earth to be with people; because he is the way to God.)

Say: ★ **Jesus' birth means God is with us. Today we're going to celebrate that fact and discover through symbols of Christmas what it means to have God with us.**

BIBLE STUDY

One Special Night (Matthew 2:1-11; Luke 2:8-20)

Say: **Let's review the Christmas story in a brand-new way.**

Before class, photocopy the "One Special Night" story (pp. 90-91). Cut apart the 15 verses and distribute them as evenly as possible among the partners.

Say: **Decide which partner will be the reader and**

which partner will lead the motions. I'll give you a couple of minutes to go over your verses together.

Have the pairs stand in a circle in the order their verse or verses fall in the story. Explain that everyone should do the motions with the pair that's performing.

Introduce the story by saying: **And now, welcome to our presentation of the Christmas story, "One Special Night."**

Lead everyone in a round of applause as the story ends. Then say: **If you could be anyone in the Christmas story, I wonder who you'd chose to be. Turn and tell your partner who you'd want to be and why.**

Allow a few moments for partners to talk, then ask volunteers to share what their partners said.

LIFE APPLICATION

Symbols of Christmas

Say: **There are so many wonderful things about the Christmas story! We look forward to hearing it year after year. There are also lots of wonderful Christmas symbols and traditions we enjoy. Let's have some fun learning more about them.**

Distribute photocopies of the "Symbols of Christmas" handout (pp. 94-97).

Choose volunteers to read aloud the explanation and Bible verse on or near each symbol. Then distribute scissors and have participants cut out the symbols.

Have partners or families use the symbols to create Christmas banners from construction paper or felt.

Decide whether you'll have each family make a banner or if you'll have each participant make his or her own banner. Even if individuals make their own banners, it's helpful to have them work in pairs so they can share ideas and work out problems together. Be sure that younger students are paired with older students or adult helpers.

Students or families will need 11×17-inch rectangles of construction paper or felt for their banners. Have them fold the rectangles in half and cut a pointed bottom 4 inches deep as shown in the margin illustration on page 92. Provide red, green, white, blue, yellow, gold, and brown construction paper or felt. Participants can trace around the symbol pattterns on

TEACHER TIP

Consider backing the "Symbols of Christmas" handout with poster board, then cutting out the shapes. Participants can take turns tracing around these sturdier shapes.

One Special Night

(from Matthew 2:1-11; Luke 2:8-20)

1 In faraway Bethlehem one special night,
  tired shepherds watched over their sheep.
  (Rest cheek on hands.)
  Then the sky was suddenly filled with light,
  and the shepherds awoke from their sleep.
  (Sit up and look startled.)

2 "Good news I bring you," the bright angel said,
  "news that will fill you with joy:
  In Bethlehem-town, in a dark cattle shed,
  is born a brand-new baby boy."
  (Pretend to hold a baby.)

3 "This child is the Christ, the Savior of all.
  He'll be in a warm manger bed
  (pretend to pull up a blanket),
  wrapped in soft clothes, this baby so small,
  with straw to pillow his head."

4 Then suddenly angels filled the whole sky
  (make star bursts with fingers),
  singing God's glory and praise.
  "Peace upon earth," came their song from on high.
  The shepherds stood watching, amazed.

5 Then, in a twinkling, the angels were gone.
  (Cross hands, then pull them apart.)
  The night grew cold and still.
  But the shepherds remembered the heavenly song
  as they stood on their lonely hill.

6 "Let's hurry to Bethlehem," one shepherd said
  (pump arms as though you're running),
  "to find the holy child."
  And, sure enough, there in a manger bed
  lay Jesus, sweet and mild.

7 The little sheep's "baa" and the doves' soft "coo"
  were the baby's lullaby.
  The shepherds fell down and worshiped, too
  (bow and fold hands),
  as a bright star shone in the sky.

8 "The Son of God has been born tonight!"
  (Cup hands around mouth.)
  The shepherds spread the word.

(continued)

And those who came to see the sight
(clap hands to cheeks)
could hardly believe what they heard.

9 Three wise men in a land far away
saw the beautiful star.
(Point upward.)
"It tells of a special child born today,"
they said. "We must travel far."

10 "God has sent us this special light
to guide us on our way.
(Point into the distance.)
We'll cross the desert during the night
and rest in the heat of the day."

11 So by-and-by, the wise men found
Jesus and Joseph and Mary.
Then the three wise men bowed to the ground
and said, "Take these gifts that we carry."
(Hold up cupped hands.)

12 Gold and sweet perfume they gave
and thought, "Our gifts are small.
For Jesus came the world to save
(spread arms wide);
he brings God's love to all."
(Cross hands over heart.)

13 On Christmas Eve, some people still search
for Mary's baby Son.
But he's not in a manger and not in a church.
(Shake head.)
He lives in everyone.
(Point both hands to heart.)

14 So when you see a star twinkling bright
(make a star burst with fingers),
in a crisp, quiet winter sky,
remember the gift God gave that night
and the angels that sang on high.

15 There's a gift that you can give Jesus, too.
It's not too hard to find.
To each person you see the whole year through
(pretend to point to several people),
be loving and gentle and kind.
(Give a hug.)

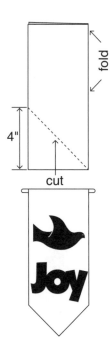

their chosen colors, cut out the symbols, then glue them in place on their banners.

If you choose to make felt banners, you may also want to supply slender dowels for hanging.

Play Christmas music as participants work on their banners. Encourage people who finish first to help others complete their banners.

COMMITMENT

Procession of Banners

When all the banners are complete, have everyone help clean up the work area, then line up for a procession of banners. Encourage everyone to sing "O Come, All Ye Faithful" as you lead the procession around the room or around the church building.

Close the procession by having everyone sit in a circle. One by one, invite participants to stand and explain why they chose to use certain symbols and what their banners mean to them.

When everyone has shared, say: **Our banners can be reminders that ★ Jesus' birth means God is with us. You may want to hang your banner in a window or on your front door. Or perhaps you'd like to give it away to someone who would enjoy its message.**

Have participants turn to partners and tell what they plan to do with their banners.

CLOSING

Christmas Greeting

Say: **Let's close our class with a special greeting.** Ask:
● **What special greeting do Christians use on Easter?** (Christ is risen; he is risen indeed.)

Say: **Let's make up a similar greeting for the Christmas season. You'll step up to someone, shake his or her hand, and say, "Jesus is born." The other person will respond, "God is with us." Let's try that together: Jesus is born; God is with us.**

Allow participants to exchange greetings with several people. Then close with a prayer similar to this one: **Dear Lord,**

92

what a difference it makes in our lives that you were born as a tiny baby long ago. Thank you for being with us. We love you. Amen.

SYMBOLS OF CHRISTMAS

The dove represents peace and the presence of God's Holy Spirit.
" 'Give glory to God in heaven, and on earth let there be peace among the people who please God' " (Luke 2:14).

Holly stays green even in winter's cold. It stands for life that never ends—Jesus' gift to those who believe in him.
" 'God loved the world so much that he gave his one and only Son so that whoever believes in him may not be lost, but have eternal life' " (John 3:16).

SYMBOLS OF CHRISTMAS

God's Son became a tiny baby who slept in a feeding box, not in a palace.

" 'Today your Savior was born in the town of David. He is Christ, the Lord. This is how you will know him: You will find a baby wrapped in pieces of cloth and lying in a feeding box' " (Luke 2:11-12).

Angels praised God and announced peace on earth.

"Then a very large group of angels from heaven joined the first angel, praising God and saying: 'Give glory to God in heaven, and on earth let there be peace among the people who please God' " (Luke 2:13-14).

SYMBOLS OF CHRISTMAS

Wise men followed the star to Jesus. The star stands for God's guidance.

"When Jesus was born, some wise men from the east came to Jerusalem. They asked, 'Where is the baby who was born to be the king of the Jews? We saw his star in the east and have come to worship him' " (Matthew 2:1b-2).

The angel announced that Jesus' birth would bring great joy to all people.

"The angel said to them, 'Do not be afraid. I am bringing you good news that will be a great joy to all the people' " (Luke 2:10).

SYMBOLS OF CHRISTMAS

Jesus is the light of the world. The candle stands for the light and hope Jesus brings to our world.

"Later, Jesus talked to the people again, saying, 'I am the light of the world'" (John 8:12a).

New Beginnings

(a lesson for New Year's or any time)

YOU'LL NEED

- ❏ foil-covered chocolate coins
- ❏ markers
- ❏ paper
- ❏ cellophane tape
- ❏ a hammer
- ❏ a bowl of charcoal chips
- ❏ a bowl of marbles or wrapped gum balls
- ❏ newsprint
- ❏ a dishpan of warm, soapy water
- ❏ a towel
- ❏ a Bible
- ❏ photocopies of the "God's Treasure" handout (p. 106)
- ❏ scissors

LESSON AIM

To help kids understand that ★ God can make us clean inside.

OBJECTIVES

Kids will
- ● tell what they would do if they were kings or queens,
- ● learn how a young king turned his people back to God,
- ● discover how God can make them clean inside, and
- ● discover that God's Word is their greatest treasure.

BIBLE BASIS

2 Chronicles 33:1–35:19

Josiah was crowned king of Judah when he was 8 years old. Both Josiah's father, Amon, and his grandfather, Manasseh, had led the people of Judah in idol worship. Manasseh's sin resulted in his capture, exile, and imprisonment by the Assyrian army. Manasseh eventually humbled himself before God, received forgiveness, and regained his kingship. On his return to Jerusalem, Manasseh ordered the destruction of idols and led the people in worshiping Jehovah God. After Manasseh's death, Amon took the throne and plunged the nation back into idol worship, sinning even more than his father had done. Amon was killed in his palace by his own officers, and the crown passed to his 8-year-old son.

Despite his tender age and the evil example set by his father, Josiah "did what the Lord said was right." When he was 16 years old, he began worshiping the true God. He rid the whole country of idols and set about rebuilding and restoring the temple. A priest working in the temple found a long-lost scroll containing the law given through Moses. When the young king heard the words of the Law, he tore his clothes in grief for the sins of his nation. The king stood in the temple and read the Law to his people, then made a covenant to follow God's commands. A short time later, Josiah led his people in the greatest Passover celebration since the time of Samuel.

Josiah was a rare leader among the kings of Israel and Judah. His dedication to God ignited a new faith and a new covenant. God used his servant Josiah to give the people of Judah a new beginning.

Psalm 51:1-2, 10

God loves to hear the repentant cry of his people. He loves us even more than he hates the rotten things we do. God always stands ready to forgive us, make us clean inside, and renew our relationship with him.

UNDERSTANDING YOUR KIDS

An 8-year-old king—boy, will your kids love that! If they were given an opportunity to rule, it wouldn't be long before they'd come up with a great agenda. Rather than "a chicken in every pot," today's kids might legislate a Walt Disney World in every state and a Nintendo in every home. What a great surprise it will be for your kids to discover that this young ruler had far greater things than amusements on his mind.

There are two positive things for your kids to discover in this lesson. The first is that kids are never too young to make a difference. The second is that when they realize they've offended God, they need to make things right immediately. God is willing to forgive their sins, both purposeful and inadvertent, and make them clean inside.

The Lesson

ATTENTION GRABBER

If I Were King

Before class, hide foil-covered chocolate coins around the room. Be sure you hide at least one for each student. To one of the coins tape a slip of paper on which you've written, "Congratulations, Your Majesty!"

Gather kids in a group and say: **I've hidden treasure all around this room. In just a moment I'll let you look for it. Don't pick up more than one piece of treasure. When you've found your piece, bring it back here and sit down. One of the treasures has a special message on it. If you find the treasure with a message, don't tell anyone what it says. Just bring it to me. Are you ready to be treasure hunters? Go!**

When everyone has found a coin, call the group together. Have the student whose coin has the special message come and stand by you. Hold up the coin and read the message to the class.

Then say: **I guess this makes you our ruler. What's your first command?**

If the child is shy or gives a command that seems inappropriate, whisper that he or she might order everyone to eat their treasure. Then ask:

● **Suppose you were suddenly to become the ruler of this country; what would you do?** (Make everyone give me chocolate; get homes for all the homeless people.)

● **How about the rest of you? What would you do if you suddenly became king or queen?** (Take a world tour; move to a palace; help poor people.)

● **What would make you a good king or queen?** (I would be fair and kind; I would tell people about God.)

● **What would make you a bad king or queen?** (If I took everyone's money; if I treated my friends and family better than everyone else.)

Say: **Believe it or not, today's Bible story is about a boy who became a king when he was 8 years old. And he turned out to be not just a good king, but a great one! This young king found a treasure, just as we found treasure here today. Let's find out about the treasure he found and what a difference it made in his life and his kingdom.**

TEACHER TIP

You might want to give the youngest children a five- or 10-second head start.

100

**The Little King Who Made a Big Difference
(2 Chronicles 33:23–34:33)**

Before class, write "The Little King Who Made a Big Difference" on a sheet of paper.

Help kids form pairs. For this activity it's not necessary to pair younger kids with older ones. Have the pairs sit in a large circle. Set out markers, sheets of paper, and cellophane tape.

Say: **We're going to illustrate this story with the quick-draw method. I'll stand in front of a pair and read a part of the story. One partner will quickly draw a picture describing what I read. Then the other partner will run to this wall** (indicate a blank wall) **and tape the picture to the wall. If I come to your pair more than once, the drawer and the taper may change roles. Don't worry about making fancy pictures; stick figures are fine. Just draw something that will help everyone remember what happens in the story.**

I'll put up the first paper with the title of our story. Who can read it?

Tape the title paper to the wall. Then read "The Little King Who Made a Big Difference" (p. 102) as you walk around the circle, pausing in front of each pair. Pace the story carefully, waiting just a few seconds between each segment. It's fine to go to the next pair as the previous pair finishes its picture and attaches it to the wall.

After the last picture is in place on the wall, invite kids to join you in front of the pictures. Have kids retell the story by explaining their pictures. Then ask:

● What made Josiah a good king? (He followed God; he made the people stop worshiping idols.)

● What was the great treasure in this story? (The book of God's law.)

● What happened when the people of Judah heard what was written in the **scroll?** (It made them realize what they'd done wrong; it made them stop sinning and begin to worship God.)

Say: ★ **God can make us clean inside. And that's just what he did for King Josiah and the people of Judah. They had gotten off to a bad start by worshiping idols. But when they found out what was right, they asked God's forgiveness and promised to obey God from then on. So the people got a fresh start.**

A new year is a fresh start for us. But God can give

The Little King Who Made a Big Difference

1. King Amon was a wicked man who taught the people of Judah to worship idols. One day he was killed by his own soldiers.

2. Then his young son, Josiah, became king. Josiah was only 8 years old.

3. Josiah worked and studied hard. He wanted to be a good king. When Josiah was 16, he began to worship the true God.

4. Josiah told the people to destroy all the idols in the land. The people obeyed their young king.

5. Josiah ordered the priests to rebuild and repair the temple. Everyone worked hard to make God's house a beautiful place again.

6. One day a priest who was working in the temple found a scroll that had been lost for many, many years. God's laws were written in the scroll.

7. The priest took the scroll to young King Josiah. When Josiah heard God's laws, he knew that his people had broken every law. He felt sad.

8. Josiah called the people to the temple and read God's laws so everyone could hear. The king promised to obey the Law. The people promised to obey, too.

9. Josiah and the people felt sad that they had disobeyed God. When God saw that they were sad and heard their promises to obey, he forgave their sins and made them clean inside.

10. Josiah was one of the greatest kings of Judah. He treasured God's Word and loved God with all his heart and soul and strength.

us a fresh start any time. Let's see what we can do to make a fresh start like Josiah did.

LIFE APPLICATION

Sad for This, Glad for That

Before class, hit a few charcoal briquettes with a hammer so they shatter into small pieces. Place the pieces in a bowl. Put glass marbles or wrapped gum balls in a second bowl. You'll need enough charcoal chips and marbles or gum balls for each student to have two of each.

Set the bowls together in the center of a table. Place a sheet of newsprint in front of each bowl. Have a dishpan of warm, soapy water and a towel nearby, out of sight.

Say: **When we want to make a fresh start, it's good to stop and think about the good things we've done, as well as the bad things.**

Stand in front of the table and have kids form a line behind you. Pick up a marble or gum ball and say: **I'm glad that I** (name one good thing you did this year). Drop the marble or gum ball on the sheet of newsprint.

Then pick up a charcoal chip and say: **I'm sad that I** (name one thing you did that you felt sorry about.) Drop the charcoal chip on the other sheet of newsprint.

Turn and face the kids. Say: **I'd like you to do just what I did. If you want to, you can just say, "I'm glad that . . ." and "I'm sad that . . ." and then finish the sentences in your head. Or, you can say what you did out loud. It's up to you. Either way is OK.**

After everyone has been through the line once, invite kids to go through the line again if they wish. It's fine if some kids choose to go a second time and others choose not to. You may want to lead the second round as you did the first.

Then gather everyone around the table and ask:

● **What happened to your hands when you named the things you were sad about?** (The charcoal turned them black; they got dirty.)

● **How does it feel to have charcoal on your hands?** (Icky; I want to get them clean.)

● **How is that like how it feels to have sin in your life?** (You feel bad about it.)

Say: **Listen to these verses from the Bible.** Read aloud Psalm 51:1-2, 10.

Set out the dishpan of warm, soapy water and the towel. Have kids take turns washing and drying their hands. As

103

TEACHER TIP

Practice folding the treasure box two or three times before class. You may want to train two or three students to be helpers. Take heart—making the box is much simpler than it looks! It's based on the familiar "salt cellar" or "May basket" pattern many kids are familiar with.

1.

2.

3.

4.

5.

6.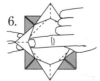

children put their hands in the water, have them repeat Psalm 51:2 after you: "Wash away all my guilt and make me clean again."

When everyone has washed and dried their hands, say: **Doesn't that feel better? Just as the soapy water cleaned our hands, ★ God can make us clean inside. Then we're ready for a fresh start, just like King Josiah and the people of Judah.**

Promise kids that they can take their gum balls or marbles home after class.

COMMITMENT

God's Treasure

Ask:

● **Who remembers what treasure helped Josiah and his people make a new start?** (The book of God's law.)

● **Why is God's Word a great treasure?** (Because it teaches us about God; because it tells us what God wants us to do.)

Say: **We're going to make treasure boxes to remind us of the new beginning God gave the people of Judah and the new beginning God is willing to give us when we ask him to forgive our sins.**

Distribute photocopies of the "God's Treasure" handout (p. 106) and scissors. Have kids cut out and roll the scroll containing Psalm 51:1-2, 10. Then demonstrate how to cut and fold the treasure box. The box can be made from the square pattern on the handout or from a 6-inch square of wrapping paper.

Have kids write their initials on the bottom of the finished treasure boxes then tuck the scrolls inside.

CLOSING

Treasures to Keep

Have kids stand in a circle holding their treasure boxes. Ask:

● **What will these treasure boxes remind you of?** (That God can make us clean inside; that God can give us a fresh start; that God can take away our sins.)

Say: **Let's bow our heads and pray a prayer of thanks because ★ God can make us clean inside.**

Pray: **Dear Lord, thank you for the treasure of your Word. Thank you for taking away our sins and making us clean inside. And thank you for giving us a fresh start. In Jesus' name, amen.**

Encourage kids to tell their families about their treasure boxes then to keep the treasure boxes as reminders that God can make them clean inside.

GOD'S TREASURE

1. Fold the square diagonally both ways, then open it flat with the plain side up.

2. Fold all four corners to the center.

3. Turn the square over and fold all four corners to the center again.

4. Fold all the points outward so they extend beyond the square.

5. Turn the square over. Fold the center points back to the outside points.

6. Pinch each top point from the outside, causing the points to stand up and fold at the top.

"God, be merciful to me because you are loving. Because you are always ready to be merciful, wipe out all my wrongs. Wash away all my guilt and make me clean again. Create in me a pure heart, God, and make my spirit right again" (Psalm 51:1-2, 10).

A Little Love and Kindness 12

(a lesson for Valentine's Day or any day)

LESSON AIM

To help kids understand that ★ God wants us to be kind and loving.

OBJECTIVES

Kids or families will
● discover how it feels to depend on others,
● hear Naomi's story,
● make gifts of kindness and examine practical ways to show God's love, and
● commit to showing kindness to others.

BIBLE BASIS

Ruth 1–4

The book of Ruth is a wonderful story of selflessness and generosity. It's so beautifully and concisely written that you could practically read the whole book aloud to your class. Read it again yourself and be inspired by God's love interpreted in simple acts of kindness.

The story of Ruth shows us that God can use everyday people to accomplish great things in his kingdom. Ruth was a Moabite, not a Jew. Yet because of her devotion to a sad old woman, Ruth became an ancestress of King David and of Jesus.

YOU'LL NEED

❏ star stickers
❏ blindfolds
❏ a box of doughnuts
❏ an adult to play the role of Naomi (optional)
❏ a robe for a Bible costume
❏ scissors
❏ markers
❏ tape
❏ photocopies of the "Hearts of Kindness" handout (p. 115)
❏ photocopies of the "Someone Cares Pop-Up Card" handout (p. 116)
❏ glue sticks
❏ a photocopy of the "Love and Kindness Mix" instructions (p. 113)
❏ ingredients for the mix
❏ a Bible

NOTE

This lesson works well with an intergenerational class. You may wish to invite whole families to join you for this session.

107

Ruth gave up everything that was familiar to her to accompany Naomi back to Bethlehem. She trusted herself to the living God who honored her sacrifice and blessed her greatly in return.

Proverbs 14:21, 31
It has been said that kindness is the language of love. Those who make it a point to be kind are God's everyday heroes. Acts of kindness done in the name of Christ are the building blocks of the kingdom of God. And no one has to wait to be old enough to participate.

UNDERSTANDING YOUR KIDS

Kids are preoccupied with many things. Kindness isn't usually one of them. Kids understand the value of being popular or good at sports or being identified with the right group of friends. But only a few kids recognize the importance of being kind to everyone, regardless of circumstance.

A classic example is what happens in school lunchrooms. Suppose a group of friends squeezes around one table, but one child is left out and has to sit alone. How many of the kids in your class would leave the group to sit with the one who is left out? We hope that some would. But most would probably think, "Whew—I'm glad I'm not the one stuck at the other table!"

Use this lesson to help kids see that God wants us to make kindness a priority—and that he blesses us in surprising ways when we do.

The Lesson

ATTENTION GRABBER

Help Me! Help Me!
Place star stickers on kids (and adults) as they arrive. Put a sticker on the shoe of the first person, on the cheek of the second person, and on the hand of the third person. Continue in this manner so one-third of the participants have shoe stickers, one-third have cheek stickers, and one-third have hand stickers.

Say: **Quickly form trios. Each trio needs one person with a shoe sticker, one person with a cheek sticker, and one person with a hand sticker.**

Give three blindfolds to each trio.

Say: **In your trios, tie the ankles of the person with the shoe sticker. Then blindfold the person with the cheek sticker. Finally, tie the wrists of the person with the hand sticker.**

When all the trios have completed this task, say: **Before class, I put a box of doughnuts in the church kitchen** (or any other place that's some distance from your room). **If you'd like to go help yourself to those doughnuts, you may. But you can't untie yourself or remove your blindfold. I think I'll go get a doughnut for myself.**

Leave the classroom without further comment. Technically, all of the participants can get to the doughnuts despite being tied or blindfolded—they can feel their way or hop. Supervise the participants to keep them from running into anything as you watch to see which trios cooperate and which try to go it alone. Then return to the classroom and take the doughnuts with you. Have participants remain tied or blindfolded as they enjoy their doughnuts and discuss these questions.

● **What went through your mind when I told you to help yourselves to the doughnuts in the kitchen?** (I was mad that my ankles were tied; I thought I'd never be able to get there; I wondered if I could find my way.)

● **How did you feel if your trio members left you behind?** (I worried that they wouldn't take care of me; I trusted them to bring me a doughnut.)

● **How did you respond when some trios started helping each other?** (I was glad I was part of a trio that worked together; I told my trio members that we should work together, too.)

● **What were the rewards for working together and taking care of one another?** (We all got doughnuts; I didn't have to feel guilty because I had a doughnut and no one else did.)

● **How was being blindfolded or having your feet or hands tied together like what happens to people in real life?** (Some people have accidents or diseases that blind them or make it hard for them to get around.)

● **If you had to stay tied or blindfolded for a month, how would you want other people to treat you?** (I'd want to do most things for myself; I'd be glad to have other people help me.)

TEACHER TIP

It's fine to have one or two groups of four. Encourage a good mix of ages in each group.

Say: **People have all kinds of difficulties in life—physical problems, losing a job or a home, failing at school—anything can happen. At times like that we need one another, just as you needed your trio members in this activity.** ★ **God wants us to be kind and loving. Let me introduce you to an old woman from the Bible whose life was turned around because someone was kind and loving to her.**

BIBLE STUDY

Tears to Laughter (Ruth 1–4)

You may want to have a woman from your congregation dress in a Bible costume and visit your class to present "Naomi's Story" (p. 111). Or, quickly put on a costume and read the story yourself. Do it with a sparkle in your eye and a twist of Jewish humor. It's great fun for kids if a man presents the story in a falsetto voice.

Lead participants in a round of applause for Naomi.

Have participants return to their trios to discuss the following questions. Pause after each question to allow for discussion.

● **What terrible things happened to Naomi?** (Her husband and sons died.)

● **How would you feel if you were the only one left in your family?** (Really sad; lonely.)

● **Why do you think Ruth went back to Bethlehem with Naomi?** (Because she felt sorry for Naomi; because she was a kind person.)

● **What good things happened because of Ruth's kindness?** (Ruth found a husband and had a baby; Naomi had a family again.)

● **When Ruth went with Naomi, do you think she expected any of these good things to happen? Why or why not?** (No, she only thought about helping her mother-in-law; she probably trusted God to take care of her but didn't know about all the good things that would happen.)

Wave your hand to get everyone's attention, then bring everyone together. Say: ★ **God wants us to be kind and loving. Sometimes God gives us great surprises, like he did in today's story. But sometimes our reward is just the happiness we feel for having done something kind.**

Naomi's Story

I've had a sad life, I tell you—a very sad life. But the living God has given me joy again! Do I look like a sad, old woman? Well, I'm not. I should say not! For God has filled my empty arms with a beautiful baby boy. A grandson! Can you believe it? A grandson born when my husband and sons were all in their graves. Let me tell you how it happened.

I grew up and married in the town of Bethlehem. When food was hard to find, my husband and my two sons and I moved to the land of Moab. Our sons married women from Moab, and for a time I was very happy.

But then my husband and sons died. I had no one left but my two daughters-in-law. I wailed and cried as they buried those men who were so dear to me. I felt empty. Empty and alone. So I decided to return to Bethlehem.

I told my two daughters-in-law to stay in Moab and find new husbands. One stayed behind. But Ruth insisted on going with me.

"I'll go wherever you go," she said. "Your people will be my people, and your God will be my God."

You should've seen the looks on the faces of my old friends when we arrived back in Bethlehem. "Can it be Naomi?" they asked. I told them how empty and lonely I felt. No husband. No sons. Bah! What good is a lonely old woman?

But there was Ruth. Why should she stay with her old mother-in-law? She's one in a million, that girl.

It was harvest time, so Ruth went out into the fields to gather grain the workers left behind. The owner of the field was kind to her. "Come gather grain in my field every day," he said.

And who should that kind man be but Boaz—a close relative of mine. I knew Boaz would sleep by the piles of grain, to guard them. So I told Ruth to put on perfume and her best clothes and lie at the feet of Boaz. When Boaz awoke and found Ruth at his feet, Ruth said, "You are my relative. Will you take care of me?"

Ah, that Ruth. She's a lovely girl. Boaz decided to marry her and buy the land that belonged to my sons and my husband. That was nearly a year ago. And just last week, my grandson was born.

All my friends laughed and cried like a bunch of old hens. "Praise the Lord who gave you this grandson," they prayed. "May he become famous in Israel. He will give you new life and will take care of you in your old age because of your daughter-in-law who loves you. She is better for you than seven sons, because she has given birth to your grandson."

So who wouldn't be happy? Praise to the living God who fills me with joy!

Love and Kindness to Go

Say: **Turn to your trio members once more. Take turns telling about a time when someone noticed that you were sad and did something kind to help or encourage you. Listen well, because in a moment you'll get to share what you heard from someone in your trio.**

Allow a couple of minutes for sharing. Then wave your hand to get everyone's attention and invite volunteers to share what they learned.

Say: **Now tell your trio members about someone you know who seems sad or discouraged, someone who could use some special love and kindness.**

Allow two or three minutes for sharing. Then wave your hand to get everyone's attention and say: **There are lots of ways to show love and kindness to people who are sad or discouraged—people in your own family, people at church, at school, or in your neighborhood. Let's have fun finding out how we can show love and kindness to all kinds of people.**

Choose one, two, or all three of these "Love and Kindness" learning-center ideas. Each is easy to prepare and fun for both kids and adults. (Consider photocopying the handouts on colored paper or stationery.)

● **Hearts-of-Kindness Coupon Center**—Participants make personalized kindness coupons to give away in decorated hearts. Set out photocopies of the "Hearts of Kindness" handout (p. 115), scissors, tape, markers, and a finished sample.

● **Heart Pop-Up Card Center**—Participants make pop-up cards with encouraging messages to send to people who are sad. Set out photocopies of the "Someone Cares Pop-Up Card" handout (p. 116), scissors, glue sticks, and a finished sample.

● **Love-and-Kindness Mix Center**—Set out bowls of cinnamon heart candies, peanuts, and shredded coconut. You'll also need a small scoop for each bowl, sandwich bags, and ribbon. Photocopy the instructions below and set them out with the ingredients.

Love-and-Kindness Mix

Put a few cinnamon heart candies in a sandwich bag. Then add a scoop of peanuts and a scoop of coconut. Tie the bag with a ribbon, then give it to someone who would appreciate your gift of kindness.

Introduce the learning centers. Allow participants to choose where they'd like to begin. Encourage adults and older kids to work together with younger kids to help them complete their projects. If you have plenty of time, let participants do the projects at all three centers. Or, offer to send home photocopies of the handouts they didn't have time to complete.

As participants work, circulate among them and ask:

● **Who's the lucky person you're going to give this to?**

● **This looks great! Where are you going to mail it?**

● **Do you have plans for sharing this with someone?**

Announce when there are three minutes of working time left, then two minutes, then one. When you call time, have participants gather their projects and return to their trios.

COMMITMENT

Gifts of Kindness

Say: **Show your trio members one thing you made. Then tell who you're going to give it to, and why you chose that person.**

Allow trios to share. Then wave your hand to get everyone's attention. Bring everyone together and ask:

● **How did you feel as you worked on projects that you knew would brighten someone's day?** (Warm and happy.)

Have a volunteer read Proverbs 14:21, 31.

● **Why is it important for Christians to be loving and kind?** (So we can show God's love; because we care about people; because it honors God.)

Say: ★ **God wants us to be loving and kind. The little gifts of kindness you've made today are just the beginning. God can show you many people who need your encouragement and love throughout the week.**

CLOSING

Blessing the Gifts

Ask everyone to hold a gift of kindness they made as you pray: **Lord, thank you for the beautiful story of Ruth and Naomi. We pray that you'll bless the gifts of kindness we made today. May they bring comfort and joy. We ask these things in Jesus' name, amen.**

HEARTS OF KINDNESS

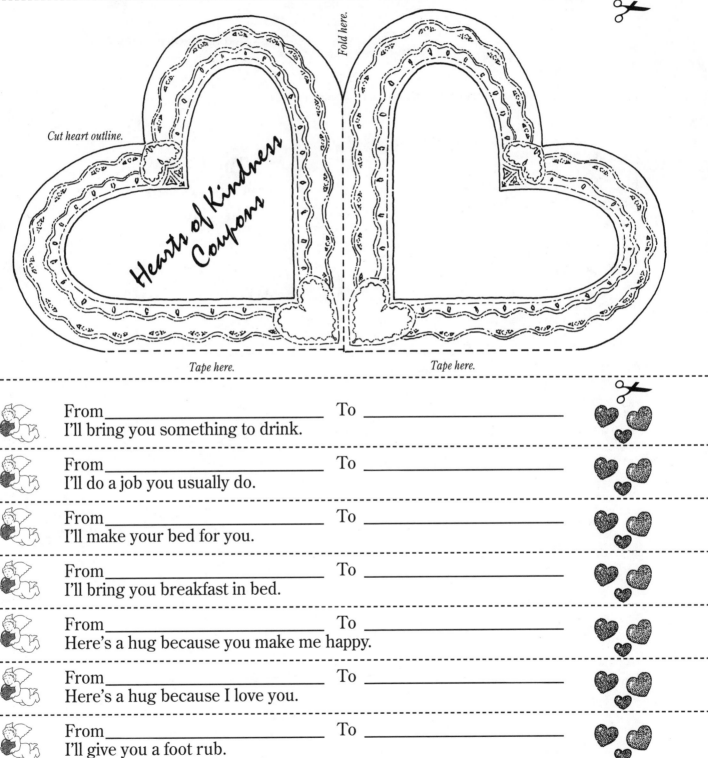

Cut heart outline.

Fold here.

Hearts of Kindness Coupons

Tape here.   Tape here.

From_____ To _____
I'll bring you something to drink.

From_____ To _____
I'll do a job you usually do.

From_____ To _____
I'll make your bed for you.

From_____ To _____
I'll bring you breakfast in bed.

From_____ To _____
Here's a hug because you make me happy.

From_____ To _____
Here's a hug because I love you.

From_____ To _____
I'll give you a foot rub.

SOMEONE CARES POP-UP CARD

Fold on the dotted lines.

1. Cut out the outside of the card.

2. Cut out the heart pop-up section and fold on the dotted lines.

3. Rub a glue stick on the back of the top and bottom hearts.

4. Place the point of the folded heart into the center of the fold of the card and press.

5. Voilà! When you open the card, the hearts pop up!

Cut heart outline. →

The Lord says, "I have loved you with an everlasting love; I have drawn you with loving-kindness" (from Jeremiah 31:3, NIV).

Cut card outline.

Fold here. →

Jesus Lives!

(a lesson for Easter or any time)

LESSON AIM

To help kids understand that ★ God's resurrection power is with us today.

OBJECTIVES

Kids will
- try to break free from licorice ropes,
- learn how Jesus broke the bonds of death,
- discover the power in kernels of popcorn, and
- see how God's power can change everything.

BIBLE BASIS

John 20:1-18

John 20 is filled with poignant vignettes in which Jesus' love and invincible power touch his followers at their most hopeless, vulnerable moments. We see those closest to Jesus pass from overwhelming loss to hopeful wonder to heart-searing joy. In the garden, Mary Magdalene wanders in confusion and pain so wrenching that she doesn't even recognize the risen Jesus. He simply speaks her name: "Mary." The sound of his voice stirs recognition and immediately banishes oppression and fear. It isn't over after all—death is the loser, Christ is alive, and all is right in God's world!

We all have reason to mourn in our lives. We all have things to fear. Injustice and tragedy break our hearts. Hunger, poverty, and disease don't go away. Evil people control terrible instruments of destruction. *But all of these are nothing compared to God's power.* There may be times when we wan-

YOU'LL NEED

- ❏ ropes of red licorice
- ❏ a trick candle
- ❏ matches
- ❏ a Bible
- ❏ a glass of water
- ❏ unpopped popcorn
- ❏ plastic eggs
- ❏ a popcorn popper
- ❏ photocopies of the "Resurrection POWer!" handout (p. 124)
- ❏ markers
- ❏ scissors
- ❏ tape or glue sticks
- ❏ a bowl

der confused, like Mary. There may be times we rub our chins in doubt, like Thomas. Crawl into the pages of John 20. Walk in the garden with Mary. Listen for the Savior to speak your name. *It isn't over after all—death is the loser, Christ is alive, and all is right in God's world. Hallelujah!*

Ephesians 1:19-20

Satan mustered all his formidable powers to try to defeat the crucified Christ. What happened on Golgotha was a battle far more cataclysmic than any human war. But the very gates of hell crumbled when Jesus broke death's chains and burst from the grave to life everlasting.

This same power is at work in us! It's a concept that's hard to take in. We don't need to tremble in the face of tragedy or evil. We are agents of the living God, empowered by the same irresistible force that raised Christ from the dead. Wow.

UNDERSTANDING YOUR KIDS

All kids feel powerless from time to time. It's one of the most frustrating feelings of childhood. And it's what draws many kids into gangs.

To kids, one of the most important parts of growing up is gaining control of their lives. They want to choose their own interests and activities, decide what to do with their money, and determine where and with whom they'll spend their time. Kids are drawn to gangs because gangs seem to spell instant power. In reality, what kids see as power becomes self-perpetuating bondage.

Use this lesson to help your kids see that they can belong to the most powerful "gang" of all time—God's gang! And that since "nothing, nothing, absolutely nothing" can stand in the way of God's power, they can do great things for God.

The Lesson ATTENTION GRABBER

Breakout Power

Have kids form trios.

Say: **Find out which person in your trio will volunteer**

to go through a test of strength. It doesn't have to be the biggest or strongest person—this is just for fun. Who's comfortable trying a strength test?

Have the people who offer to do the strength test hold their arms in front of them, fists together. Give the other members of each trio two ropes of red licorice.

Say: **Wind the licorice ropes around your brave volunteer's wrists. Volunteers, when your wrists are all wound up, you can try to break free. Wait until your partners have you all tied up. OK—let's see what happens.**

Cheer for all the volunteers as they try to break the licorice ropes. Have trio members help their volunteers by unwinding the licorice ropes one loop at a time until all the volunteers are able to break free. Then give everyone a big round of applause and allow kids to share the licorice.

Ask the volunteers:

● **How did it feel to be tied up with licorice?** (Silly; kind of fun.)

● **What was it like trying to get free?** (Frustrating; fun; embarrassing.)

Ask the other trio members:

● **What went through your minds as you cheered on your volunteer and loosened the licorice rope?** (I hoped he would break free; I wanted to be encouraging.)

Say: **Our Bible story today is about someone who was able to break free from one of the most powerful forces in the world. Let's see how it happened. Follow me.**

BIBLE STUDY

Life in a Dark Place (John 20:1-18)

Before class, explore your church to find a room you can darken completely to tell the story of Jesus rising from the dead. Place matches and a trick candle in your pocket or in a small bag. Take your Bible, this book, the candle, and matches with you as you lead the children to the place where you'll tell the story.

Gather children in a circle in the darkened room, open the Bible to John 20, and ask:

● **Who can tell me about how Jesus was crucified?** Allow several children to contribute to the story. Draw out information with questions such as "Why did the Jewish leaders want to kill Jesus?" and "Why did God let Jesus die?" Fill in any important information kids leave out. Then ask:

TEACHER TIP

It's important that this be an exciting experience, not a scary one. You may want to leave the door open a crack and have younger children stand near it.

● If you'd been Jesus' follower, what would you have done after they took Jesus down from the cross and buried him? (I would've run away; I would've cried.)

Say: **Friends who wanted to take care of Jesus' body couldn't do it because it was dark and time for the Sabbath day of rest. But Mary Magdalene came back early on Sunday morning to put burial spices and perfumes on Jesus' body.** Ask:

● **What do you think it was like to come to a dark tomb?** (Scary; quiet.)

Say: **Well, Mary expected the tomb to be quiet and dark, but that wasn't the case. The stone was rolled away, and the tomb was empty. Mary ran back and told Peter and John.** Ask:

● **What did Mary think had happened to Jesus' body?** (She thought someone had come and taken it away.)

● **But what had really happened?** (Jesus had risen from the dead.)

Light the trick candle. Ask:

● **Did anyone expect Jesus to rise from the dead? Why or why not?** (No, because they didn't understand God's plan; no, even though Jesus told them he would rise from the dead, they didn't understand.)

Invite someone to blow out the candle. Ask:

● **What about the soldiers and Jewish leaders? Did they think Jesus was gone for good? Why or why not?** (Yes, because they didn't understand God's power.)

As you wait for the flame to relight, say: **Mary didn't know what to think. Peter and John went back home, but Mary stayed by the tomb crying. Suddenly two angels appeared in the tomb and asked why she was crying.** Ask:

● **What would it be like to suddenly see two angels in a dark tomb?** (Surprising; kind of scary; they'd probably be bright.)

Say: **Then Mary turned around and saw a man standing in the garden. The man also asked why she was crying. Mary asked, "Did you take him away, sir? Tell me where you put him, and I will get him." The man said "Mary." Suddenly Mary recognized the man.** Ask:

● **Who do you think it was?** (Jesus.)

Say: **You're right! Mary said "Teacher!" Mary wasn't sad or frightened any more. She found out that God's power is greater than anything—even death!**

Return to your classroom, carrying the candle. Ask:

● **How was Jesus' rising from the dead like what this candle does?** (Trick candles surprise us when they light again after we think they've gone out, and Jesus surprised people because no one thought he could live again after he'd died.)

Invite a child to dip the candle in a glass of water. Then ask:

● **How was Jesus' resurrection different from this trick candle?** (The candle can be put out with water, but nothing can make Jesus die again.)

Say: **Earlier today some of you tried to break out of licorice ropes.** Ask:

● **Do you think any of you could break away from the power of death?** (Not without God's help.)

Say: **Before that first Easter, no one had ever risen from the dead by his or her own power. But now we don't need to be afraid of death's power anymore because God's power is stronger than death. God's power is stronger than anything. And ★ God's resurrection power is with us today.**

LIFE APPLICATION

Easter Egg Hunt

Before class, fill plastic eggs about one-third full of unpopped popcorn and hide the eggs around the room or an open area in the church. If possible, have one egg for each student.

Say: **Let's find out more about God's resurrection power by going on an Easter egg hunt. When you find an egg, don't open it! Just bring it back here. You may bring back only one egg. Ready? Go!**

You may want to give younger students a few seconds' head start. When everyone returns with an egg, invite students to sit in a circle on the floor and carefully open the eggs. Ask:

● **What's inside your eggs?** (Popcorn.)
● **Is it alive?** Allow children to disagree.

Invite students to pour a few kernels of popcorn into a popcorn popper. Turn on the popper.

Then say: **Well, let's see.** Examine a handful of popcorn. **It doesn't squeal when I pinch it. There's nothing green or growing. There's no heartbeat. I don't know— I guess it's not alive.** Ask:

● **What happens when this popper gets hot?** (The popcorn pops; we can eat the popcorn.)

TEACHER TIP

If the eggs don't close tightly, you may want to tape them shut.

TEACHER TIP

If you have an air popper, you might want to remove the top and let the popcorn fly into the air and let kids try to catch it.

Say: **It's amazing to me that God put inside each of these hard little kernels the ability to pop into fluffy, white popcorn. And God puts special power in each of us, too, when we believe in Jesus.** Read Ephesians 1:19-20. Ask:

● **How is God's power in us like the power in a kernel of popcorn?** (We can't do anything special without God's power, and the popcorn can't pop unless it gets hot; popcorn does surprising things, and when God's power is in us we can do surprising things, too.)

Say: **Let's nibble on our popcorn and celebrate the fact that ★ God's resurrection power is with us today!**

COMMITMENT

Poppin' Power

Put the lid on the popcorn popper and invite kids to pour the rest of their popcorn kernels into the popper. Keep it on until everyone's popcorn is popped. As the popcorn pops, ask:

● **How did the disciples use the resurrection power God gave them?** (They told everyone about Jesus; they started the church around the world; they healed people.)

● **Did God's resurrection power make the disciples strong and brave? Explain.** (Yes, because they weren't even afraid of the people who killed Jesus; yes, because they kept telling others about Jesus even when some disciples were killed or put in prison.)

● **Can God's resurrection power make you strong and brave? Explain?** (Yes, because with God on my side I don't have to be afraid of anyone; yes, because I know that God's side will win in the end.)

● **How can God use his resurrection power in you?** (God can have me tell others about Jesus; God's power can make me loving and kind; God can use his power in me to solve problems in the world.)

Pass out photocopies of the "Resurrection POWer!" handout (p. 124), markers, scissors, and tape or glue sticks. Pair older kids with younger ones.

Say: **We'll use these handouts to make bags for our popcorn. But before we do that, write or draw on the front of your bag one way you think God might use his resurrection power in you. Then tell your partner about what you wrote or drew.**

Help kids make bags according to the instructions on the handout. Encourage partners to help each other. Pour the popped popcorn into a bowl as kids are working on their bags.

CLOSING

Sharing the Power

Have kids line up in front of the popcorn bowl. As you scoop some popcorn into each child's bag, say: ★ **God's resurrection power is with us today!**

Have kids stand in a circle with their bags of popcorn. Drop a plastic egg into each person's bag. Ask:

● **What part of the Easter story can the empty egg remind us of?** (The empty tomb.)

● **What can the popcorn and the bags remind us of?** (God's resurrection power is with us; God's power can make anything happen.)

Say: **When you go home, tell your families about the egg and the popcorn and the bag. And be sure to share some popcorn with them, too!**

Close with a prayer similar to this one: **Dear Lord, only a great, great God could raise Jesus from the dead. Thank you that Jesus lives! Thank you for the power you have for our lives today. Help us to serve you well. In Jesus' name, amen.**

RESURRECTION POWER

A. Write or draw on the front of the bag one way you think God might use his resurrection power in you.

B. Cut out the bag.

C. Fold and tape.

D. Fold up the bottom.

E. Push in the corners.

F. Fold the edges over and tape.

G. Pinch and crease the sides at the bottom.

RESURRECTION POWER

"And you will know that God's power is very great for us who believe. That power is the same as the great strength God used to raise Christ from the dead" (Ephesians 1:19-20a).

Quick Programming for Children's Ministry

Messages for Children

Donald Hinchey

Captivate and challenge young listeners—with Bible-based sermons just for them. Each creative message uses language kids readily understand—so you'll teach meaningful lessons on topics such as…

- God's love,
- faith,
- putting God first,
- forgiveness,

…and dozens of other topics. Plus, each talk uses involving activities to grab and hold kids' attention—so they'll remember the truths you present.

You'll also get seasonal ideas for helping children understand the meaning of…

- Advent,
- Easter,
- Pentecost,
- Christmas,

…and other important days. You'll use these lessons for children's moments in Sunday worship—or at camps, retreats, and other special events.

5-Minute Messages for Children

ISBN 1-55945-030-4

6-Minute Messages for Children

ISBN 1-55945-170-X

Quick Group Devotions for Children's Ministry

You'll discover 52 lively Bible-based devotions for elementary-age children—the best devotions from 20 veteran children's workers from across the country. No dull sermonettes here, but active, experential lessons that kids will enjoy AND remember. Each touches on a Bible topic you want to teach like…

- complaining,
- honesty,
- friendship,
- God's love,
- prayer,
- overcoming temptation,

…and over 40 more! Plus, you'll find holiday devotions for New Year's Day, Valentine's Day, Easter, and Christmas. Perfect for Sunday school, children's church, vacation Bible school, day camps—any time children need to learn from the Bible.

ISBN 1-55945-004-5

Interactive Learning Resources from *Group*®

Interactive Bible Stories for Children

You can tell captivating Bible stories when you use these books! These over-sized storybooks help children *experience* Bible stories. Interactive questions and motions draw children into the Bible and bring the stories to life. They'll run from the Egyptians with Moses and the Israelites. They'll talk about what it would be like to be swallowed by a fish. They'll climb into an imaginary boat and go fishing with Peter and the disciples. And they'll talk about what it would have been like to be healed by Jesus.

These books are easy to use, too. Storytellers simply choose a story, sit down with children, and start to read. Interactive motions and questions are built right into the story.

Plus, everyone—children and adults—will love looking at the beautiful illustrations.

Interactive Bible Stories for Children: Old Testament
ISBN 1-55945-190-4

Interactive Bible Stories for Children: New Testament
ISBN 1-55945-291-9

When-It-Happened Bible Timeline Posters

Decorate your Sunday school and Christian education rooms and teach the Bible at the same time! These new, full-color Bible Timeline posters display important Bible events in chronological order with fun, clever illustrations.

And they're huge—12" x 60" each!

Each highlighted event includes Scripture references to encourage children to dig into the Bible for more. And kids love studying the amusing illustrations. Parents will love these posters for their children's rooms, too!

When-It-Happened Bible Timeline: Old Testament
ISBN 1-55945-193-9

When-It-Happened Bible Timeline: New Testament
ISBN 1-55945-194-7

BRING THE BIBLE TO LIFE FOR YOUR 1ST THROUGH 6TH GRADERS WITH GROUP'S *HANDS-ON BIBLE CURRICULUM*™

Energize your kids with Active Learning!

Group's **Hands-On Bible Curriculum**™ will help you teach the Bible in a radical new way. It's based on Active Learning—the same teaching method Jesus used.

Research shows that we retain less than 10 percent of what we hear or read. *But we remember up to 90 percent of what we experience.* Your elementary students will experience spiritual lessons and learn to apply them to their daily lives! And—they'll go home remembering what they've learned.

In each lesson, students will participate in exciting and memorable learning experiences using fascinating gadgets and gizmos you've not seen with any other curriculum. Your elementary students will discover biblical truths and <u>remember</u> what they learn—because they're <u>doing</u> instead of just listening.

You'll save time and money too!

While students are learning more, you'll be working less—simply follow the quick and easy instructions in the **Teachers Guide**. You'll get tons of material for an energy-packed 35- to 60-minute lesson. And, if you have extra time, there's an arsenal of Bonus Ideas and Time Stuffers to keep kids occupied—and learning! Plus, you'll SAVE BIG over other curriculum programs that require you to buy expensive separate student books—all student handouts in Group's **Hands-On Bible Curriculum** are photocopiable!

In addition to the easy-to-use **Teachers Guide**, you'll get all the essential teaching materials you need in a ready-to-use **Learning Lab**®. No more running from store to store hunting for lesson materials—all the active-learning tools you need to teach 13 exciting Bible lessons to any size class are provided for you in the **Learning Lab**.

Challenging topics each quarter keep your kids coming back!

Group's **Hands-On Bible Curriculum** covers topics that matter to your kids and teaches them the Bible with integrity. Switching topics every month keeps your 1st- through 6th-graders enthused and coming back for more. The full two-year program will help your kids...

> ◆ make God-pleasing decisions,
> ◆ recognize their God-given potential, and
> ◆ seek to grow as Christians.

Take the boredom out of Sunday school, children's church, and youth group for your elementary students. Make your job easier and more rewarding with no-fail lessons that are ready in a flash. Order Group's **Hands-On Bible Curriculum** for your 1st- through 6th-graders today.

Order today from your local Christian bookstore, or write: Group Publishing, Box 485, Loveland, CO 80539. For mail orders, please add postage/handling of $4 for orders up to $15, $5 for orders of $15.01+. Colorado residents add 3% sales tax.